Sedona Survival Guide

Comical Wild West Spiritual Adventures

Dusty RedStone

Copyright © 2018 by Dusty RedStone
All rights reserved. This book or any portion thereof
may not be reproduced or used in any manner whatsoever
without express written permission of the author,
except for the use of brief quotations in a book review.

Printed in the United States of America

First Printing, 2019

ISBN - 9781790918850

www.DustyRedStone.com

Dedication

This book is dedicated to anyone who is suffering with debilitating chronic illness. Especially for those with "invisible illness" that no one else can see, but you sure can feel. As someone with Multiple Connective Tissue Disorder, celiac disease, Sjögren's syndrome, Chronic Lyme disease, and some others, I "see you." I hope this wacky book gives you a reason to laugh today.

Acknowledgements

Thank you to my parents for your help, you made the impossible possible.

Thank you to my amazing wife for always laughing with me, even when everyone else shakes their head in disapproval...

Thank you to Catherine McAfee for her editing contributions.

Disclaimers

The content in this book is for entertainment purposes only. It is NOT a how-to-guide on ANYTHING. **Do not try anything in this book at home.** Meant for Mature Audiences Only

Please Note: Public Nudity and Recreational Marijuana are ILLEGAL in Arizona.

The term "Pretendian" is used in the context of bringing attention to non-Native people who deceive the public, commit cultural mockery, and sell ceremony under false pretenses.

Many of the stories and events are satire. All the stories are based on actual events that took place on a different timeline in an alternate dimension. Some are actually from my past lives. All names and descriptions of people have been changed to ensure privacy. Any likeness or resemblance to anyone living or dead is coincidental. I do not condemn or condone any particular person, business, or service in Sedona, the surrounding areas, world, dimension, or universe.

Some of the stories in this book are a bit rude, crude, gross, and totally bizarre. The purpose is not for trashy shock value. I would rather you, the reader, perhaps get shocked while reading a story, rather than find yourself in an uncomfortable and unexpected situation.

Adopting the Ostrich as your "spirit animal" keeps your head protected in the sand at the expense of your exposed butt waving in the breeze.

Warning: Stoner Discretion is Advised. Reading this book while high may cause you to pee your pants from laughing too hard.

Table of Contents

Preface...1

Author Background 4

About the Author's Spirit Guide and Life Coach..............................6

Introduction to Sedona...8

Mini-Glossary..13

The Sedona Survival Kit...15

Chapter 1..18
What is a Woo-Woo?

Chapter 2..22
Words of Wisdom: Interviews with Four of Sedona's Finest

Chapter 3..29
Vortexes, Hiking, and the Wild Lands of Sedona

Chapter 4..44
Yard Sales and Estate Sales: Windows of the Soul

Chapter 5..56
New Age Nursery School

Chapter 6..61
UFOs and Aliens

Chapter 7..64
Bigfoot, Aliens, Marijuana, and the Cloak of Invisibility

Chapter 8..69
Psychics, Channelers, and Mediums

Chapter 9..76
Is Practicing Yoga Cultural Appropriation?

Chapter 10..80
Gluten-free Cultural Appropriation

Chapter 11..84
Vegans, Colonics, and the "Toothless Wonder"

Chapter 12..89
Making Friends in Sedona is Hard to Do

Chapter 13..94
Sedona Social Media

Chapter 14..98
New Age Politics

Chapter 15..103
Do You Wish to Become a Sedona Transplant?

Chapter 16..112
Thinking of Running a Business?

Chapter 17..118
How I Uprooted and Transplanted to Sedona

Afterward..126

Extended Glossary (Super Spiritual Version)...................................127

One Last Thing...138

Preface

Before I take you for a wild ride on a whirlwind of vortex energy into a magical world of absurdity and hilarity, I would like to be serious, just for a couple of pages. Then we can get on the spaceship to the vortex and hang out with Bigfoot, I promise. We are living in a time where people are so disconnected and divided. We have lost the ability to find commonality with the oldest social lubricant: no, not tequila, but laughter. All around the world there is one linguistic sound that unites us. "Ha" is the universal sound of laughter and coincidentally it is also used in Traditional Chinese Medicine as the sound to heal the heart. It does not matter where you are from; we all laugh the same. I can still remember a time when phones did not isolate us and politics did not make us all hate one another.

I have had many Near Death Experiences (NDEs), not too many to count, but too many to remember the exact number off the top of my head. One of those experiences was a weeklong hospital stay where I was on and off my deathbed. Obviously, I recovered and I am still here driving my family crazy. This book is not about those experiences. It is a topical overview of Sedona and a collection of absurd Woo-Woo stories to make you laugh and feel good.

On a serious note, a close family friend had an aggressive form of cancer and she did not recover. The end was slow and painful for her; she was completely bedridden. Out of the many, many visitors she had, she chose to take the time to send me a thank-you email before she passed on. The thank-you note was not for flowers, candy, or my sympathy. I did bring her those things, but more importantly, I also brought her something that cannot be held, something no one else brought her: a smiling face and my really bad sense of humor. Unconsciously, all of her other visitors came from a place of sadness. She let me know how much it raised her spirit and helped her that day to have one last opportunity to laugh, smile, and just enjoy the moment.

Receiving that email from my dying friend that day lit a spark inside of me. I remembered how much I enjoyed making my classmates laugh in school when I was a pain-in-the-ass class clown growing up. I always thought laughter was just confirmation of my stupidity and foolishness. Never in my wildest dreams did I think that my lack of an etiquette filter could bring comfort and joy to a dying friend on one of the worst days in her life. Thankfully, I took the chance of being comedic at what seemed like a very inappropriate time.

Certain local events, including the "Sedona Sweat Lodge Incident" in October of 2009, an increase of local suicides, and reports of questionable behavior among certain spiritual groups in Sedona, have all attributed to an air of sadness in this small town. It is not uncommon for ill-equipped hikers to go missing or for tourists and locals alike to need helicopter rescues from places like Bell Rock. Obviously, not everything that happens in Sedona is a laughing matter. With that being said, sometimes the only remedy for a dire situation is a good belly laugh.

In case you did not know, Sedona is a town where "healers," gurus, and yoga teachers have manifested into abundant numbers. I personally enjoy the diversity of thought, wild theories, and out-of-the-box thinking that is the culture here. I often peruse local social media sites for daily anecdotal amusements and updates on the latest UFO or Bigfoot sightings.

One morning, I was surprised and saddened to see some very negative posts by a local man. Like me, he was out of work due to disabilities caused by chronic illness, but unlike me, he had no support system. Among other things, he was expressing his surprise at the irony of the situation. He was in a town jam-packed full of metaphysical light workers and he could not find any relief. Nor could he afford it, for that matter.

I became an online friend of this gentleman, even though I was really unsure if I would be able to help him in any way. Alas, I am not an interdimensional time traveler or a reincarnated Shaman. As time went by, his online postings became darker and darker. As is common in the New Age culture, this poor guy was met with a barrage of comments that consisted of regurgitated psychobabble: "focus on the positive," "you must heal yourself," "love yourself or no one else will love you," "become a god and transcend human suffering." I am not a super spiritual "Empath" or "Sensitive," but as a fellow human being, I could empathize with his pain and the frustration of being patronized.

Instead of offering my new online friend words of wisdom or encouragement, I offered something a little different. At the risk of looking like a juvenile fool, I started posting memes of poop jokes, fart jokes, and other ridiculousness on his timeline. At first, I received some "likes" from him, then hearts and laughter emoji's. Then one day I received, as the New Agers would say, "an affirmation from the Universe." I woke up to a comment that the depressed man wrote on one of my posts that read, "You are freaking hilarious! I love your posts. They always make me laugh and brighten my day." Anyhow, I think you get the point; laughter has been and most likely always will be the best medicine.

As of late, I often think about that online friend of mine when I see people having meltdowns and attacking each other on television and social media. It has become so easy for people to hate one another without really knowing who they are. The political spirit animals known as Elephant and Donkey have made almost everyone lose their sense of humor. I am sure that some of the stories in this book will piss some people off, offend, or whatever. My hope is that for the most part, they will make people laugh.

On a broader scale, I really hope I have done my small part to make laughter contagious again so that people can get back to laughing together, regardless of their differences. Who knows, if you choose to laugh, you may meet your new best friend. I do not care if you are on the left, the right, a human, an alien, a Bigfoot, or an interdimensional traveler; we all laugh the same.

I heard a very profound statement recently: "Do not worry about those who you offend, worry about those who are deceived because you withheld the truth."

That is way too deep for this book. After this point, we probably will not get out of the wading pool.

Instead, I would suggest, "Do not worry about those who you offend, worry about those who are sad because you held back your sense of humor."

In the spirit of the sacred clowns, or the Heyoka as the Lakota call them, let us open our hearts with laughter.

Welcome to Sedona!

Author Background

(*Sarcasm Alert*)

I am the most enlightened author in the world. You are blessed to have found this book. The fact that the universe manifested this for you is an affirmation that you are fulfilling your soul mission. You will quickly see that my experience as a life coach, yoga instructor, Reiki healer, light worker, Starseed, psychic, guru, keynote speaker, alien channeler, manifestation expert, soul retrieval specialist, animal intuitive, Shaman, and ascended master is a priceless gift that should be exalted.

Dusty RedStone is my European name. My Sedona name is Dusty ThunderFlats, short for Dusty Thunder Flatulence. The skunk is my spirit animal. I was bestowed these honors by a Sedona Pretendian, Chief Squatting Dog. He took me on a spirit journey where it was discovered that aliens were channeling messages through my farts. The messages could only be deciphered by my dogs. Fortunately, I am an animal intuitive and I was able to receive the alien messages by reading my dogs' minds. That is how I "received" the knowledge in this book to share with other sentient beings. For the past ten years, I have lived aboard a time-traveling light ship learning the secrets of the universe. I just returned and I was age-reversed so it actually appears as if I never left.

I hope you know I am obviously kidding, but sometimes amidst the absurdity of Sedona, it is very hard to tell. In actuality, my dogs think I am very cool. Everyone else I know would agree I am more than a little hard to handle, maybe even a bit of a pain in the ass. I moved to Sedona ten years ago and had no idea what I was in for. I was almost burned alive in a sweat lodge at a New Age center before I even heard of Sedona. I spent plenty of time chasing rainbows and unicorns hoping to find a pot of gold. I have been through the New Age ringer for sure. I think for the most part I am no worse for wear, probably even better off as a result. If I poke fun at something in this book, there is a better than average chance I have tried it somewhere along the way.

I unknowingly brought Lyme disease with me from Connecticut to Sedona. It went undiagnosed and cascaded into a snowball effect of health problems that ended my public teaching career early. In my darkest hours, I have found that comedy and laughter are in fact the best medicine. Nothing can touch hearts and open minds like a good uncontrollable belly laugh! On that note, I hope you enjoy the humorous side of Sedona. Life is too short; if you cannot save the world, then at least try to make the world laugh.

Thank you and many blessings to You, Dear Reader, as we begin our epic adventure into Red Rock Country.

I appreciate you embarking on this journey to the sacred land of Sedona. It took me a solid decade of living here to amass this collection of stories. Depending on how the stars line up, within a month or even a week in this amazing place, you may have experiences that pale mine in comparison. I have traveled to about seventy percent of the national parks in the western USA, all over the east coast, Cuba, Jamaica, and Brazil. I also worked at a sleepover summer camp with people from thirty-three different countries around the world. I can safely say that Sedona is not like any other place, at least that I have been to. The people who find their way here are equally as eyebrow raising, mostly in a good way. I know one thing for sure; I have never received more blessings, hugs, wishes of peace, and greetings of "Namaste," than I have in Sedona.

Overall, I love this town, mostly for the open-minded people, abundant wildlife, and the breathtaking views. As inconvenient as the traffic is, it is kind of flattering that the number of tourists have doubled in the last ten years. I hope one day that Sedona once again becomes an accessible place for families to live, not just to visit. Perhaps the Sedona I moved to ten years ago will somehow rematerialize and "diversity of inhabitants" will not be a term used to define the history of this beautiful place.

About the Author's Spirit Guide and Life Coach

Throughout the book, I mention my spirit guide. His name is Joint is Always Lit. He is an ascended guru master whom I know from a past life. He often joins me in physical form on my adventures. His name refers to the fact that he always has a lit marijuana cigarette. That infinite joint is what gives him his powers and abilities from the spirit world. It was poor planning on my part to attract a pot-smoking entity. He began the journey to me from far beyond the veil in my late teens when I was a big time pot-smoking connoisseur. Ironically, by the time he traveled to me on the astral plane, I had quit getting high. We are kind of an odd couple. He is unique in that he is both an elder and an ancestor, a very rare combination. I am protected by his guidance.

When Joint is Always Lit is too high to materialize, I can be seen traveling around Sedona with my life coach. My life coach is kind of like an emotional support puppy, but he is a human. He is too enlightened to use a name, so I just refer to him as my life coach. He is easily recognizable with his purple hair, handmade feather headdress, and over-sized bear paw slippers that he wears everywhere. He used to be a little shy in public, but he was cured of his social phobias after he was allowed to sit in on a women's empowerment chanting ceremony that cut the cords to his past life trauma. He can trace his ancestral lines back to some of the first Pretendians who arrived in Sedona in the 1980's and 1990's. I am truly blessed to have him in my life.

I actually have a note from my doctor stating that I need them both to accompany me in restaurants and on airline flights. I just have to make sure to clean up after them and to make sure that Joint is Always Lit does not sneak off to get high in the airplane bathroom. The good news is that they are both hypoallergenic so they do not pose a threat to other people who may have allergies. If you see them with me in public, please refrain from rubbing their heads or bellies for good luck. It disturbs their work and karma.

Satire Alert: The stories in this book actually happened. However, in an effort to protect people's identities, I did change some minor details and leave some information out. In Sedona, many people refer to their spirit guides very casually and nonchalantly; it is as if they are talking about a friend or a pet. Also, it is almost taboo to live life in Sedona without paying a life coach to keep you on track.

With this in mind, my spirit guide and life coach join me on my many adventures throughout this book. In reality, I had people accompanying me who were not interested in becoming infamous characters in this book. Fortunately, my fictitious spirit guide and life coach were more than happy to fill in for them. As I mentioned, I have had many NDEs, and I am very open-minded concerning spirituality. I also had plenty of experience with medical marijuana earlier in life, and I know many people who benefit from it. The way spirit guides and marijuana are portrayed in this book is not meant to discredit people with ties to either. On the contrary, I think both topics could benefit from a touch of humor in hopes of making them more mainstream and accepted.

Introduction to Sedona

The breathtaking scenery of Sedona will have most visitors agreeing that it is one of the most beautiful places in America. Another common consensus is that Sedona is a super spiritual Wild West sensory overload. If you have crystal phobia, you are in the wrong place. You will find crystals in unsuspecting places like professional offices of doctors, lawyers, and realtors. In a half mile stretch of retail shops in Sedona, known as "Uptown," or "Uptown Sedona," you can get your fortune told, chakras aligned, energy cleared, and even have an aura photo taken. If you manifest it, you may even get a super long, super spiritual, and super uncomfortable hug by a local. Who knows, they may even throw in an eye gazing session for good measure. Get ready to ascend to the highest plane; you have arrived!

Sedona is a place of extremes and the middle path of balance is all but abandoned. It is a magical place where fantasy and reality butt heads on a daily basis. Locals are becoming scarce, while short-term house rentals are taking over residential neighborhoods. People are not being removed by force. The beauty and popularity of the area has resulted in skyrocketing prices. Some locals claim, "Sedona will either love you or spit you out," like she is some kind of supernatural goddess. Some people actually believe that anyone who lasts more than a couple of months has "arrived" or "ascended." In actuality, surviving in Sedona has more to do with having enough "green energy," "love donations," or "energetic exchanges," all also known as cash.

The "vortex energy" has shifted the landscape dramatically. In almost any other town, the stories and characters abundant in Sedona would likely be laughed at and recognized as "performance art" or parody. In Sedona, larger than life absurdity is placed on a platform and worshipped. It is supposed to take ten years of intense practice to master a martial art. I have lived in Sedona for ten years and I would say I have not mastered living here, but I have some wild stories to tell. If you are here long enough, you will hear about things like the Mandela Effect, interdimensional travel, and alternate timelines. I wish I could go back in time and give myself this book before I moved to Sedona.

When you first disembark the magic bus, flying carpet, spaceship, rental car or teleportation beam into Sedona, you will most likely experience a cultural shock smack dab in your third eye. If you have ever been to the Las Vegas Strip, you know the feeling; it is like you are in another world. Sedona does not have any strip clubs or casinos, but there is an abundance of everything New Age groovy. After a while, it will seem commonplace to receive an aura cleansing while waiting in the checkout line at the grocery store, or to receive a sacred sage smudge kit from your realtor with instructions on how to cleanse the energy of your new abode. You may even feel like you are being rude if you do not ask new acquaintances about their past life history. If your chakras are out of alignment, do not fret. What happens on the astral plane stays on the astral plane.

A friend of mine, who lives in the northern part of the mid-west, recently asked me what to expect when he visits Sedona, since he will be passing through on a road trip. I told him that Sedona is a lot like San Francisco; many liberal open-minded people live here, but it is located smack dab in the center of a fairly conservative state. He immediately responded tongue in cheek by exclaiming, "Yay! Just like San Francisco! Does that mean that people go to the grocery store naked?" Sadly, I had to inform him that we are not quite that "San Francisco" just yet. Hiking naked, maybe; shopping naked, maybe not.

One of the first people I met in Sedona informed me that Sedona used to be an ocean, totally underwater, which is true. According to her, she was a "dolphin person," which is a reincarnated soul who used to swim in "prehistoric Sedona" as a dolphin. She then let me know that she recognized me as a dolphin person due to my energy and aura, of course. She was even kind enough to show me her birthmark between her shoulder blades, which she claimed was actually her blow hole in her past life. She handed me her business card and let me know that since I was a local, she would give me thirty percent off her normal $165 fee for a past life reading. The initial "consultation" that identified my dolphin origin story was free, on the house. I have always enjoyed practical jokes, so I laughed and asked if and how many people she had fooled with her prank. Woo-Woo! That was a big mistake! She was not joking and I was lucky I did not get slapped! Lesson learned. That is Sedona for you.

People travel to Sedona for a wide variety of reasons: to glimpse a Bigfoot or a UFO, to attend metaphysical conferences, spiritual retreats, and alternative healing sessions, and to enjoy the landscape by hiking, mountain biking, or golfing, and of course to make pilgrimages to vortex sites. If you are already totally enlightened, that is okay, there is still plenty of magic in this book for you. I have included a plethora of comedic stories from encounters I have had during the past ten years of living in this town. There is guaranteed to be something for everyone in this book, whether you are a tourist, a "transplant," a new arrival, or a longtime resident. I guarantee at the very least you that will find a few laughs.

This book is meant to provide some knowledge to help you, the reader, to understand the nuances of Sedona, thus enabling you to better enjoy your ventures while in this amazing town. By encouraging a healthy sense of caution, this book is meant to save the reader both time and money. I often see people either jump right into New Age experiences, only to waste money, or they avoid New Age experiences altogether for fear of being scammed.

I do not consider myself an "expert" in anything. I continue to wear the metaphorical white-belt, identifying myself as a lifelong student. I have walked through the New Age minefield and survived. My intent is simply to share general information and tips about the Sedona New Age experience in an amusing format.

Numerous books and movies about Sedona, spanning the past thirty years or longer, cover almost any related topic you could imagine. Topics ranging from the historical perspective of the Sinagua "No Water People" and the first white settlers, to vortexes, aliens, yoga, Tai Chi, crystals, magic, and of course, hiking. What seems to be lacking is a perspective of what it is actually like to move to and live in Sedona. Not as a settler, or psychic, or a hiking guide, but as a semi-normal everyday person. Someone who is open-minded, yet grounded, could offer some perspective into navigating this Wild West tourist town. Since no one like that existed, I went on a vision quest and channeled my twin soul from an alternate timeline to find some answers.

I have ten years of wild, crazy, funny, and sad stories to share from one of the wackiest places on earth. Anyone who is promoting Sedona as a boring retirement community or a family-friendly vacation destination simply does not want to scare people away. Conversely, anyone who characterizes it as a Woo-Woo Wonderland, hosting some of the most spiritually evolved people, aliens, and interdimensional beings, is probably exaggerating a wee bit as well. Somewhere in between lies the "Real Sedona." I will tell you, it has been a wild ride living here.

If you are looking for people to tell you that Sedona is a mystical utopia that will magically "manifest" all your wishes without any effort, then you can find them a dime a dozen. They will most likely charge you an arm and a leg, but they will call it a "love donation" or an "energy exchange." If you do not see results, it will somehow be your fault. Sound familiar? If so, then you have probably been taken for the ride along the "Manifestation Highway." According to legend, Sedona will only be magical if you believe it to be so.

Sedona is not like anywhere else. Everyday life here is far from normal. People from all over the world visit Sedona, creating crowds and traffic jams in what was once a small, peaceful community. The hellacious amount of traffic that comes through this once small town during tourist season is growing every year. Ten years ago, estimates indicated that about two million tourists visited Sedona annually. That number is now closer to four to six million, depending on the source. The biggest worry in Sedona once was making sure to smoke your Sativa weed during the daytime, and then to smoke your Indica weed after dinner so that you would not pass out at 4:20. Those concerns have been replaced with learning to use parking meters and navigating roundabouts.

Sedona used to consist of mostly Woo-Woo people; now they are hard to find. The Sedona that so many fell in love with was like a flower child of the 1960's, with a name like Rainbow Moon Sedona, who would drop acid with her boyfriend, while running around topless and barefoot in the moonlight, her skirt dancing in the breeze. It was not uncommon to see her eating dinner at four a.m. in an all-night diner, while her boyfriend named Tre sold pot out of his motorcycle saddlebags. It is as if our beloved Rainbow Moon Sedona went off to college and returned as Ms. RM Sedona, PhD. She now wears pant suits and is engaged to, but not living with, her life partner Spencer. She stays "connected to her roots" by going to a farmer's market once a month and vaping CBD. In other words, she has become kind of boring and sold out.

    I applaud anyone who is willing to think outside the box regarding his or her life journey. Sedona is a great place to learn and grow. Just keep in mind that Sedona is not another planet or alternate dimension. The same rules apply here, as they do anywhere else. Many will try to sell you the idea that Sedona is a magical wonderland, superior in every aspect to anywhere else. It is certainly an amazing place, but a lot of clever marketing has gone into selling the illusion that it is "*the only place*" in regard to spiritual sacred land.

    If you are brand new to Sedona or to the New Age experience, I would recommend reading this book in its entirety before visiting. So many people have closed their hearts to the New Age of Sedona based on fear and hatred of the unknown. On the other hand, many people come here with their hearts and minds wide open. Unfortunately, wallets also open quickly, coaxed by the eagerness to be healed or to be blown away by mystery and intrigue. Laughter is a great way to open your heart to a world you may have otherwise ignored, or to pump the brakes a little bit before you jump into a New Age "sweat lodge." Get woke! After all, you will not buy Bullshit once you can identify a Bullshitter!

Mini-Glossary (Extended Glossary located at the end of the book)

Recently, I was in Uptown Sedona where I witnessed an incident that arose from the use of the term "Aho." In Lakota, the term translates to "Hello," and in Kiowa, it translates to "Thank You." In the New Age culture, "Aho" is used more as an affirmation, similar to "Amen" or "So be it." AnyWoo, back to the incident in Uptown Sedona, a tourist was lost and a local hippie New Ager guy was giving her directions. At the end of their discourse, the lady thanked the young man, to which he replied, "Aho." The lady gasped, reflexively slapped the man across the face, and exclaimed, "I ain't no ho!" She proceeded to pummel him with her hiking poles as he fell to the ground in the fetal position. Fortunately, I was able to intervene and explain to the tourist that the poor guy meant no harm. The lady gave the man a sizeable love donation to apologize for the misunderstanding, and then all was right once again in Sacred Sedona. After this tragic event, I knew that there was a very big need to enlighten tourists and to share the meanings of Sacred Sedona New Age vocabulary.

I have put the most essential survival terms in a mini-glossary in the beginning of this book. In addition, you may wish to read the extended glossary at the back of the book before proceeding into the chapters, in order to build your New Age vocabulary bank. If you are already at a much higher level of enlightenment, you may wish to use your intuition to decipher what meaning best resonates with you.

The glossaries in this book are not in astrological or alphabetical order. Instead, one term flows into the next, in a synchronized cosmic event. This glossary is meant to be read from start to finish; the definitions flow into one another... Enjoy.

Essential Sedona Survival Terms / Guru-splaining:

(super spiritual slang words and phrases translated to layman's terms)

Crystal Healing – get a bunch of crystals and see what happens

Atheists – people who do not believe in crystals or vortexes

Holding Space – having a conversation

Grace – making it through yoga class without farting

Veil – wall that separates earth and spirit realm, also known as sobriety

New Age – so much more evolved and on a higher vibrational frequency than the Old Age

Asstrollogy – a specialized practice in guided meditation designed to help victims who were trolled by an asshole on the Internet

Vibrational – who the heck knows for sure

Vibrating at a Higher Frequency – pretending to be in a good mood

Had a Calling – did not jive with working 9 to 5; decided to go to India and study yoga

Common Sense – a very rare and elusive phenomenon

Normal – a group of people who became extinct in Sedona in the late 1980's

Blessed – ability to manifest lots of "love donations" and "green energy"

Love Donations / Green Energy – cold, hard cash

Intuitive – can determine what people had for lunch simply by smelling their breath

Animal Intuitive – think "crazy cat lady" on steroids and peyote

The Sedona Survival Kit

A visit to Sedona requires some intensive soul work on both the astral and physical planes of existence. It is highly advisable to put together a Sedona Survival Kit as you prepare to venture to Red Rock Country. Your karma and chakras depend on your due diligence. You may feel moved by spirit to include some personalized items, but I have listed the bare essentials you need in order to ensure a successful Super Spiritual Wild West Adventure.

Essential Super Spiritual Items to Include in Your Kit:

Medicine Bag – necessary for membership in the Sedona Pretendian Tribe and to keep your Sedona Survival Kit organized

Pretendian Tribal Name – a made-up name for Non-Native Americans, such as "Quacks Like Duck," "Balding Eagle," or "He Who Stepped on Frog." Helps break the ice and create mystery. People will not be sure whether to ask you about your spiritual heritage or to simply laugh.

Soul – necessary for your journey, but they often get lost. If that is the case for you, make sure to go to a soul retrieval session ASAP.

Salt – essential for cleansing crystals

Sage – sometimes vegan food can make you fart; sage really purifies the air and creates harmony

Compass – will not work around vortexes, thus proving to skeptics the vortex energy is real

Tribal Tattoo – will let others from your tribe recognize and welcome you

Essential Oils – showering often is frowned upon; we have to save water for our 18th generation. Essential oils to the rescue!

Sarong – a man skirt that is essential for any fashion-forward New Age gentleman

Man Bun – keeps away mosquitoes and those pesky successful women with high IQs

Toe Rings – important for your toes to feel affirmations that they are as valued as your fingers

Convincing Past Life Back Story – no one in Sedona has only lived once. You must choose a great make-believe persona for Sedona street credit.

Spirit Guide – you will be lost in Sedona without one, so choose wisely

Life Coach – effects of marijuana in Sedona are multiplied by a 1,000 fold due to the vortex energy. A life coach is the only way to avoid Couch Potato Syndrome.

Wind Chimes – you want to make sure to annoy your neighbors so you can complain about how mean they are

Crystals – you must have a huge collection; crystal withdrawal is painful and should be avoided, lest your aura suffers

Shamanic Certificate – never leave home without one; going rate is $500

Reiki – yes, we have leaves to pick up in the fall

Water Bottle Full of Urine – I saw on a survival show that if you run out of water you can drink urine. I always go prepared with a pre-filled bottle in case I do not have to "go." Legend has it that urine is a natural form of bug spray that may also repel scorpions and other humans.

Reiki Certificate – necessary to restructure the urine, so it is "safe" to drink

Warning – do not use crystals in your water bottle for purification or restructuring; they are a choking hazard and bad karma. Also, do not actually drink urine or "sacred" Sedona water you find while hiking.

Tantra Books – if your girlfriend, boyfriend, life partner, soul mate, or twin flame catches you looking at porn, you can just tell them it is "research to supplement your tantric reading material."

Aura – important to color coordinate with your twin flame. Also, never leave the house with a white aura after Labor Day.

Magnifying Glass – necessary to read the bar codes on food packaging labels while grocery shopping. Also, you will want to telepathically communicate the bar codes to cashiers, so they do not have to scan your food items with the laser bar code readers.

Genetic Testing Kit – even as much as 1/1,000,000,000,000,000 actual Native American ancestry is like hitting the New Age genetic lottery

    If you need further assistance organizing a Sedona Survival Kit, I will be happy to assist you during a live chat for the low price of $1,987.00 in love donations. Or, I can just put a Sedona Survival Kit together for a green energy exchange in the amount of $9,999.99, plus the cost of shipping and sage smudging fees.

Chapter 1

What is a Woo-Woo?

Survival Tip: If someone is "holding space" for you, do not worry. You are not on line for anything; they are just having a conversation with you.

Even after living in Sedona for ten years, "What is a Woo-Woo?" is a hard question to answer. For starters, "Woo" is essentially anything metaphysical or paranormal. "Woo-Woo" tends to refer more to the outlandish way people talk and present these topics as part of the New Age lifestyle. Some people embrace the Woo and refer to themselves playfully as "out there in Woo-Woo land." Other people use the term "Woo-Woo" in a derogatory sense, as a description of those who "bring shame to Sacred Sedona."

I think we all have a little Woo in us, but there are many different levels for sure. I have narrowed it down to six basic groups. Some people move fluidly from one to another and some are pretty cemented in a specific group. I decided to use common styles of dress categories to illustrate and describe the groups, but they have little to do with clothing. Almost everyone in Sedona dresses casually. I have seen real estate agents hosting an open house in sweat pants. My wife was initially thrilled about the "freedom to wear whatever you want in Sedona." I quickly burst her bubble when I began wearing kung fu pants everywhere.

The following categories are metaphorical and based on an individual's level of comfort when embracing their inner and outer Woo-Woo.

Level 1 – Zero Woo detectable – Black Tie / Evening Gown: These are mostly retirees who moved to Sedona with big bucks and have no interest in metaphysical New Age topics at all. Many of them are very nice people who are here for the views, weather, and golf. Some are quite intolerant of the Woo-Woo free spirit crowd. You might refer to them as having a stick up their butts, or as it is known in Sedona, a crystal lodged in their Toot Chakra.

Level 2 – Lowest level, barely any Woo detectable – Business Casual: They might loosen up their metaphorical tie or take off their heels and sit a moment to "humor" the idea that there is more than meets the eye "out there." Maybe they have been to a few yoga classes and received a Reiki treatment once or twice. They may have even ordered a gluten-free pizza or had a psychic reading.

Level 3 – Medium Level, a touch of Woo – Casual /Jeans and T-shirt: They most likely came to Sedona to be around the outdoor recreational activities, as well as alternative healing, healthy lifestyle, and open-minded people. They probably have a good understanding of the New Age culture and are likely metaphysical enthusiasts. Perhaps they are a little shy talking about Woo-Woo topics in public, but they are non-judgmental and eager to learn and grow. They are usually grounded, have what is considered a semi-normal life and normal job, and may or may not work in the New Age industry.

Level 4 - Medium to High Level of Woo – Slippers and Pajamas in Restaurants / Bathing Suits to the store: These folks often have some really good stories to share and lots of Woo-Woo experience. They are more than willing to share stories, but you may have to get to know them a bit before the really wacky stuff comes out. As their "dress" implies, they are completely fine letting the world know that they are totally into the New Age school of thought. They most likely work in a New Age field or are heavily involved in New Age culture. There's not a lot left to the imagination after meeting them, but they are usually somewhat grounded on planet earth.

Level 5 - The Highest Level of the Woo - The Nudists: As the name implies, some of these folks actually may be caught hiking naked in the forest. However, the name is mostly metaphorical. These folks will just let it all hang out there from the get-go. They will blurt out upon meeting you in person, or even publicly post on social media, their entire galactic or interdimensional resume, leaving nothing to the imagination. In the first five minutes of meeting a Level 5, you will most likely hear about

UFO sightings, Bigfoot encounters, and their telepathic communications with aliens. Some of these folks are the shy type of nudist who walks around with a newspaper to cover up their naughty parts. On the other hand, you may meet the type who will do the propeller dance in front of a crowd. What is the propeller dance? I am glad you asked. I will answer by sharing the following story.

When my family first moved to Sedona, we lived in a condo in the Village of Oak Creek (VOC), which had a community pool and hot tub. We would often use the pool and hot tub after dinner to stargaze, listen to crickets, and to look for UFOs flying by. One night when the moon was full, a new face appeared: a rather portly fellow wearing a towel wrapped around his waist. Without warning, he closed his eyes, tore off his towel, and revealed his birthday suit to everyone present. Joint is Always Lit was disgusted and instantly hid behind the veil. My life coach, on the other hand, was too shocked to move; he just stared in disbelief.

The Level 5 Woo-Woo Nudist specimen did not jump into the pool, at least not before his ritual. He began chanting and then locked his hands behind his head and started rotating his hips around like he was hula hooping. He did not have a hula hoop, but he did have a knack for getting his ding dong to swing around in a circle like an airplane propeller, hence the name.

A young lady shrieked in terror exclaiming, "What the heck are you doing?"

The man stopped his routine abruptly, took a deep breath, and glared at the woman. He replied, "I am using the energy of the moon to supercharge my reproductive prowess. My girlfriend is fertile and we were sent to earth to have a moonchild. One day he will become the sovereign protector of this planet and will usher in an age of peace."

That was definitely a visual I would like to forget, but hey, if the moonchild is bringing peace, then maybe it was worth it. After that visual trauma, I had to go to therapy for six weeks, hold space for five days, and go to three soul retrieval sessions before Joint is Always Lit would materialize again.

As I mentioned, most nudists are only metaphorically nude, not literally nude. I think you get the idea. Even beyond the nudists, there is even a more super spiritual level, "The Chameleons."

Level 0 – The Chameleons: They usually have reached higher levels of Woo, but they have the ability to stay grounded and to use discernment to blend into whatever crowd they find themselves. Based on the many people I have met over the years, I think there are probably quite a few Chameleons in Sedona and in the New Age community in general. Chameleons will usually match the mannerisms, speech, and topics of conversation of the people around them, in order to keep others comfortable. I fall into this level. I have experienced almost everything considered Woo-Woo except a Bigfoot sighting. However, I am usually able to find some common ground with whatever level of Woo I encounter. If you saw me or another Chameleon in the grocery store, you would probably think we were just boring, everyday people.

When you visit Sedona, which type of Woo-Woo will you meet? Who will you identify with? Will you become a Chameleon and blend in, or will you let it all hang out? It is important to consult your guru to make sure that you are on the right spiritual path. For example, if you are not yet willing to become a vegan, you should try to get a life coach to convince you to convert. Otherwise, you will never reach a high level of Woo. Everyone knows that the flatulence of carnivores repels spirit guides, while vegan farts manifest bliss and good karma.

Chapter 2

Words of Wisdom: Interviews with Four of Sedona's Finest

Survival Tip: If knowing is half the battle, then do not wager your green energy on a winning outcome.

When word got out that I was writing this book, I was contacted by many locals who wished to be interviewed. I narrowed the requests down to five finalists: Mary Moon Child, Genghis Con, Ah Sol, Venus Luna Tic, and Itchee High Knee. Unfortunately, a top contender, Mary Moon Child, "had a calling" and was unable to be interviewed because she was away on a soul quest. It was all meant to be, and the following interviews are a result of divine synchronicity.

Interview with Genghis Con, a local Sedona Shame-man

Me: "Good morning sir. Thank you for agreeing to this interview."

Genghis Con: "Namaste. Do you mind if I read your aura?"

Me: "Whatever boats your float."

Genghis Con: "Your aura is telling me that to avoid a karmic debt; you would be wise to gift me 200 love donations for this interview."

Me: "We talked about this. No love donations."

Genghis Con: "Green energy exchange? No? Okay."

Me: "So, Genghis Con, what led you to become a "Shame-man?""

Genghis Con: "Well, I really like the ladies, but I do not resonate with the nine-to-five grind. I could not find a sugar goddess, so I had to find a way to accumulate monetary blessings."

Me: "Did you study with a master?"

Genghis Con: "Yes. I paid a guy I met online 500 bucks, I mean love donations, for a Shame-man certificate."

Me: "Fascinating. Can you describe some of your services?"

Genghis Con: "Yoni massages are my specialty, but I also do some soul retrieval stuff and I chant to a drum. In addition, I make a mean Ayahauseca brew."

Me: "Have you had any affirmations about your calling or life purpose?"

Genghis Con: "Absolutely! I have manifested an abundance of blessings, green energy, and goddesses."

Me: "Do you have any words of wisdom for our readers? Or perhaps you can share a daily mantra?"

Genghis Con: "Hmmm? I always say, "The more you get paid, the more you get laid.""

Me: "Interesting. Any last thoughts you would like to share?"

Genghis Con: "Yeah, don't let "The Man" control you. Be a free spirit. Trust the *you-niverse* to provide what your soul needs. Whatever you focus on is what you will attract: love, peace, and manifestation. Namaste."

Me: "Thank you so much for your time and insights."

Genghis Con: "Hey, do you have like five bucks for a burger? If you give me a ride to yoga class, then I'll share this joint with you. It's some good shit!"

Interview with local guru, Ah Sol, a self-proclaimed "living sun god"

Me: "Nice to meet you. How long have you been in Sedona and what brought you here?"

Ah Sol: "I have been here for three months. I was led here by my spirit guides. There are many students who need my help."

Me: "What do you teach your students?"

Ah Sol: "I simply remind them what they already know: the universal laws like the law of attraction and focusing on the positive."

Me: "So you are charging thousands of dollars for those friendly reminders?"

Ah Sol: "The energy exchange is suitable and mutually beneficial."

Me: "Regarding your two girlfriends, what role do they play in your business and your life?"

Ah Sol: "They bear witness to my great works. They have been selected to carry my children, "the chosen ones." Prophecy states that my offspring will save the world."

Me: "From what belief system did this prophecy originate?"

Ah Sol: "Belief is subjective; the prophecy is written. I am a god. I came here from another planet to do my good works on the earth plane."

Me: "We have an email here from your ex-wife. She claims that she left you when you blew her life savings on prostitutes and cocaine. She also says that you battled depression when you found out you have a low sperm count and cannot conceive children."

Ah Sol: "Wha-wha-what? I mean, those are lies and delusions of a very jealous woman. She was holding back my spirit quest and soul purpose."

Me: "Your ex-wife also claims that you used to cry at night hugging a teddy bear."

Ah Sol's two girlfriends chimed in, "Wait, is this all true? What about the "chosen" babies we are supposed to have, Ah Sol?"
After that, we had to end the interview. Ah Sol had a complete meltdown and admitted he was a total sham. He confessed he was in fact infertile and that he was just using the two women for their money and to feed his sex and cocaine addictions. Despite Ah Sol's confessions becoming local news, many of his followers remain in heavy denial and still maintain his status as a "living god."

Interview with a local UFO, Alien, Bigfoot, and Crystal Expert: Venus Luna Tic, with a PhD in "Asstrollogy"

Me: "Good morning. Thank you for sitting down with me."

Venus Luna Tic: "It is my pleasure, Starseed."

Me: "Excuse me?"

Venus Luna Tic: "You must know you are a Starseed. I see it in your chakras."

Me: "No, that is news to me. Anyway, how did you get involved in your field?"

Venus Luna Tic: "I received a divine calling from Gaia, the Earth Mother."

Me: "Can we start with crystals? Anything you would like my readers to know?"

Venus Luna Tic: "Crystals have memory. They connect the past to the present, and they allow us to see the future."

Me: "How about UFOs and aliens?"

Venus Luna Tic: "I actually work with many of the Star People on the Asstral Plane."

Me: "Have you ever been aboard an alien ship?"

Venus Luna Tic: "Of course, I am a regular contactee. Frequently, I do not recall an experience until much later. I have actually had sexual intercourse with a few aliens. I have alien-human hybrid children with at least three different species of aliens."

Me: "Have you met your space children? Do you miss them?"

Venus Luna Tic: "Oh yes, I see them every day. I am telepathically communicating with them right now."

Me: "How about the Bigfoot? Any human-Bigfoot babies out there?"

Venus Luna Tic: "Are you mocking me?"

Me: "Of course not. This is incredible testimony. You are very brave and courageous."

Venus Luna Tic: "No. Bigfoot does not mate with humans. Their DNA is much too pure to mix with humans. Bigfoot is actually much more spiritually evolved than humans."

Me: "How has Bigfoot stayed so elusive over the years?"

Venus Luna Tic: "This may sound far-fetched, but Bigfoot actually uses marijuana smoke to maintain invisibility. They only show themselves to "test" humans."

Me: "I have actually heard that before. Have you ever gotten high with a Bigfoot?"

Venus Luna Tic: "Now I know you are mocking me. This interview is over."

Interview with Sedona Pretendian and Healer: Itchee High Knee and his spirit guide, Sting Key Fin Gar

Me: "Great to meet you, Itchee High Knee. How did you get your name?"

Itchee High Knee: "I identify as a member of the Sinagua Indians who once inhabited this sacred land."

Me: "You know the Sinagua tribe vanished hundreds of years ago, right?"

Itchee High Knee: "Minor detail. The tourists and hippie chicks don't know any better. Wait, you won't print that, right?"

Me: "I will be tasteful in my decision of what to print."

Itchee High Knee: "Cool man. I got a good thing going here. I mean, all I gotta do is put some feathers in my hair, play my flute, and sell sweat lodge ceremonies. I am making mad bank just chilling out."

Me: "No problem. How about your healing services?"

Itchee High Knee: "Yeah, I use sage, drums, and call the ancestors. My healings are profound. I have five pages of testimonials, if you want to see them."

Me: "Did the "tourists and hippie chicks who don't know any better" write your testimonials?"

Itchee High Knee: "You want to get high? This interview is getting a little too heavy. I feel like some negative energy is affecting you."

Me: "No thank you. I am good. Did you ever consider that you are making a mockery of actual Native Americans?"

Itchee High Knee: (He responded by sticking out his tongue and putting his thumbs in his ears. Then he chanted some type of Pretendian mantra.) "Na-na, Na-na, Boo-Boo, stick your head in Doo-Doo."

    He then got out some sage, lit it, and chased me out of his house.

Chapter 3

Vortexes, Hiking, and the Wild Lands of Sedona

Survival Tip: It is best to visit vortex sites after a hard and cleansing rain. You will be less likely to inherit a karmic disturbance.

One reason Sedona became a hot spot for New Age seekers is, of course, the vortex phenomena. Vortexes, in the Sedona sense, are energy points in the earth that emit energies of varying qualities. (I purposely used the plural vortexes. I have heard local "experts" argue at length that the plural is actually "vortices." Honestly, who the heck cares?) Vortexes are rumored to be charging stations for anti-gravity spaceships as well as possible power generators for portals into other dimensions. The idea of energy points along the surface of the earth is not new, but the Sedona vortex phenomenon has been advertised heavily in order to attract New Age tourists. Different civilizations around the world have prayed at energy centers long before Sedona ever had her vortexes exposed to the public. To imply that dramatic healing can and will only take place in Sedona at vortex sites is misleading. It would be akin to telling people they only have acupuncture points on their left foot, when in fact they exist all over the body.

Modern Sedona folklore includes rumors that hippies often had sex on vortexes; the resulting pleasure is known as a "vorgasm." Some people claim that a vortex sexual experience will be "the climax of your Sedona adventure." Legend also has it that someone buried very powerful magnets at vortex sites in order to show the disruptive effect that vortex energy has on compasses.

An elderly lifetime resident told me that many years ago, a local group formed and arranged for a number of spiritual people to come to Sedona who claimed they could find vortexes. The lifetime resident stated that most of these spiritual, vortex-locating people did not enjoy hiking far distances, which may explain why most of the vortex sites are located so close to roads or are found along easy hiking trails. There are numerous vortexes in Sedona, but usually only about four or five are a tourists. Methods of finding the unadvertised vortexes range from using dowsing rods to channeling messages from aliens.

According to some psychics and other spiritual types, very little to no energy remains at vortex sites. After seeing that Sedona has become overrun with tourists, perhaps some locals have attempted to stifle the excessive tourist flow by promoting the idea that Sedona vortex energies have been depleted. Even though there seems to be some validity to the idea of energy locations on earth, it seems as if they have become overly sensationalized. Vortex sites could hold the keys to the universe, or they could simply be a marketing ploy to attract tourists to Sedona.

Leave No Trace

Responsible nature enthusiasts practice the "leave no trace" ethic. As the name implies, this set of tenets promotes the practice of minimal to no impact upon the wilderness someone visits. Sharing public places, outdoors and indoors, with strangers who do not practice "leave no trace" can be a real drag. When I was in college, a gym was located in the basement of my dorm. It was very nice and professionally managed, with a large variety of equipment. At the time, I was only casually acquainted with Joint is Always Lit and had not yet met my life coach. Without their support, my college years were very difficult.

I was a member of this gym for about two years, which helped me to stay in shape and to be active. One day I was resting between sets when I saw a guy across from me seemingly daydreaming. I wish that was all he was doing. He proceeded to look off into space while he simultaneously engaged in a rather intense game of pocket pool with his right hand and booger mining with his left hand. After a couple minutes, he admired the discovery from his nose and gobbled it down. He then finished his exercise sets on the machine and walked off without wiping the equipment. After that incident, I was not as excited anymore to work out in that gym. I wish this story had nothing to do with the Sedona vortex phenomena, but alas…

A Memorable Cooling Vortex Experience

During my first summer in Sedona, I decided to check out a few vortex sites. The weather was too hot for my wife, so I ventured out with Joint is Always Lit. I hiked to a vortex rumored to have a "cooling effect." I figured, why not? It was about 100 degrees outside. If I were going to feel the cooling effect, then that would be the day.

Ten years ago, when the number of tourists was much less, it was common to have a trail to yourself, especially during the heat of a summer day. I was very excited to get to this vortex, which was only about a half mile from the trailhead. I would rather not say which vortex; I really do not want to embarrass it due to what "manifested" there.

As I crested the hill and neared the flat, open area, I could see in the distance that I was about to have company. It seemed as if someone was sitting on the red rock surface meditating in the shade. I figured it would be all good and maybe I would meet a new friend. As I walked closer, I saw a guy in his late twenties chanting loudly with his eyes closed. His chanting caught me off guard, but the fact that his pants and boxer shorts were hanging in a tree really threw me for a loop.

He noticed me looking very uncomfortable and said, "Do not worry. I am a professional."

I thought to myself, "What, a professional wacko?" I told him, "Oh, good to know. Is this the cooling energy vortex?"

He replied, "Oh why, yes it is. Have you come here to cool your root chakra and heal hemorrhoidal disturbance in your karma?"

I said, "No, I was actually just kind of hot and wanted to see if I could feel the cooling energy. I thought it would be easiest on such a hot day."

At that point, I was thinking why the heck am I still talking to this guy? "Hemorrhoidal disturbance in your karma?" Is he serious?

He proceeded to reach his hands under the sides of both of his butt cheeks to pull them apart. I was actually aware of this practice from yoga class. The stark contrast from yoga class was that we were all wearing clothes when instructed to perform this pose. Hemorrhoid Man then explained to me that he was trying to obtain maximum exposure to the ground. In order to feel the energy, one has to really connect the warmest part of the body, the root chakra, of course, unclothed to the earth."

I replied, "Well it looks like you have the best connection point and some really good energy flow there. I'll just leave you to it."

I am pretty sure he bid me a "Namaste" and then I was on my way. Needless to say, I was not too excited to revisit that vortex. Maybe I would return after a really good, cleansing monsoon rain that would clear the vortex energy of his "hemorrhoidal karmic disturbance."

I was so distracted by this strange behavior that I did not even realize Joint is Always Lit had vanished! When I realized he was gone, I hung my head in sadness. After all the time I spent healing my spirit guide after he witnessed the airplane propeller dance, I did not know if he would ever return to this plane of existence.

Fortunately, synchronicity is top-notch in Sedona. On the walk back to the car, I encountered a Shame-man. Shame-mans are kind of like Shamans, some even have real skills, but they are known to dance around naked in the woods in order to "court" young women. Fortunately, this Shame-man kept his clothes on and agreed to shape shift into a crystal in order to lure my spirit guide back to me. In no time, Joint is Always Lit was back. He was not even traumatized. Turns out his wife ran out of weed and was summoning him to get more. He snagged a huge bag from the naked vortex guy while he was distracted talking to me, and so all was well in the universe.

Except for the vortex hemorrhoid guy, I have not seen that many nudists out and about. I did know a woman who was proud to let my wife and I know that when she goes hiking, she is naked. She starts out hiking with a sundress that comes off as soon as she is in the woods. I should mention that Arizona is a very strict state regarding public nudity and indecent exposure. There are quite a few stories of people simply peeing in the woods and getting busted.

One time my life coach and I were in a trailhead parking lot getting ready to go home when this college-age hippie chick looks right at us, hikes up her hippie skirt, and then takes a nice, long hippie piss only twenty feet away from us… next to a bush, not behind a bush. Another time, we were up on Bell Rock when a lady started acting a little jumpy and nervous. Apparently, she had to "go" badly, and there was not even a tumble weed for her to hide behind. She just dropped her trousers and went. Here's the funny part: You know when your dog pees and makes eye contact with you? Well, if your dog's eye contact makes you uncomfortable, substitute your dog for a grown-ass woman staring you in the eye while she is pissing in the middle of Bell Rock trail! Whatever! We did not get bent out of shape or report her to the local authorities. Arizona should probably get the crystal out of its Toot Chakra regarding laws about peeing in the woods.

A Camera-Shy Scorpion

My hiking trail name is "Poopmaster." It is a name given to me by a supreme goddess, my wife, for my uncanny ability to identify all types of poop in the woods.

I was on a hike with my dogs and my spirit guide by Bell Rock one day when I heard a man screaming. I hurried around the bend in the trail where I saw the screaming man, apparently in excruciating pain, holding his lower back. His girlfriend quickly explained to me that he had captured a scorpion that seemed "friendly." So, the man had put the scorpion on his shoulder for a picture, only for it to get inside his shirt and sting him.

He began screaming at his girlfriend, "You gotta pee on my back or I could die!"

I tried to tell him that urine was for jellyfish stings, and that I was pretty sure that method was actually proven ineffective. He was hysterical and convinced urine was the only way to cure him. His girlfriend also seemed convinced that it would work, but she refused to do it. Then they turned to look at me and my life coach.

"Oh no!" I exclaimed. There was not a chance in Sedona that I was going to pee on this guy's scorpion bite. Bell Rock is a very busy trail and we were only a quarter of a mile from the parking lot. They looked hopefully at my spirit guide, but he was way too bashful to do such a thing. None of us had cell phone service, so I told them I would go for help. The man was in so much agony; he could not even stand up. Scorpion stings do hurt like heck and some people are deadly allergic to them. At this point, I was propositioned; he offered me $50 to pee on his back. I refused again, and then I turned around to head for the parking lot. He yelled to me that he would give me all the cash in his wallet. I considered it, but my spirit guide informed me that it would steer me off course of my soul mission, so I again declined.

Two couples came around the corner in time to hear his generous cash offer. They were curious about what was happening, so I filled them in on what was going on. One of the guys asked how much was in his wallet. The bite victim's face lit up and he ordered his girlfriend to check his wallet.

She counted and said, "He has $140. Will you do it for him?"

One of the guys shook his head no. The other guy seemed like he was going to say yes, but then chickened out. With that bad news, the bite victim crumpled to the ground and started rolling around in agony.

Then one of the ladies blurted out, "Why the heck not? $140! Tell me where I gotta pee!"

I grabbed my spirit guide and got out of there as quickly as I could. I was not interested in seeing a golden shower in the middle of Bell Rock Trail.

Encounters of the Sedona Kind

You really never know what you will encounter on hiking trails in Sedona. Stories exist about mysterious black helicopters, men with automatic rifles chasing people out of areas, and even Bigfoot sightings. I have seen the black helicopters out on the road to Palatki. They are either heading to a secret military base to collude with aliens or maybe just stopping by to refuel at the Sedona Airport. Considering the large number of legal gun owners and the open carry laws in Arizona, it may be safe to assume that rumors of armed military people out in the wilderness were merely hunters who scared some jumpy tourists. As for Bigfoot, I have never seen one. However, there is a lot of land out there and apparently gorillas were considered mythical creatures until the early 1900's. I guess anything is possible.

A school resource police officer, with whom I worked when I taught school, told me that when he was a traffic cop back east, about five percent of people he stopped had guns in their cars. In contrast, he estimated about ninety-five percent of people he stopped in Arizona had guns in their cars. Also, several gun ranges are located on National Forest land and it is common to hear gunshots in the distance.

A few years ago, a scene unfolded at our local Cottonwood Walmart that had allusions to an old cowboy movie shootout scene, the epic kind where the wagons all circle up. Anyone present would have seen the connection; the police cars formed a circle in the parking lot, as eight officers and nine suspects exchanged gunfire. Unfortunately, it ended in one of the suspect's deaths, with a police officer and another suspect injured.

Two-legged (human) perverts and rabid fox attacks can be concerns, which are the main reasons many locals carry a small revolver when hiking. Some people carry bear spray, but perverts and rabid animals may not respond to that. It is quite amusing when tourists see a local carrying a firearm on hiking trails. I have seen guys toting huge hand cannons on their hips; the tourists who see these gun-toting guys will often gasp, stare, and even snap photos.

Sedona's High Desert Climate

It is not uncommon for Sedona's winter nighttime temperatures to fall below twenty degrees. The winter of 2017 was unseasonably warm, so I only used our wood stove about ten times. In contrast, the prior winter was cold, so I used almost a full cord of firewood. We have a very small house with a big wall of south-facing windows. On a sunny winter day, our house becomes warm from the low-traveling sun. However, when the summer sun travels much higher in the sky, it leaves us alone. Summer daytime temperatures can rise above 110 degrees, creating a heatstroke threat while hiking.

South-facing architecture is an idea that modern builders modeled from the Sinagua ("No Water People"), who built cliff dwellings around the Sedona and Verde Valley areas. The Sinagua built all their stone houses on south-facing cliffs to stay warm in winter when the sun is low, and cool in summer when the sun travels too high to shine directly into dwellings.

The funny thing is the name, "No Water People," is perhaps an inaccurate name historians gave them. In general, much more water was once available in the Verde Valley area and in Arizona; an estimated ninety percent of wetlands were lost when towns and cities were built. I do not cry in the woods hugging trees, but I think that will irritate anyone with common sense!

Near the U.S. and Mexico border, the weather is warmer due to the much lower elevation. Sedona sits in a high desert with an elevation at over 4,000 feet. North of Sedona, Flagstaff has an elevation beginning at 7,000 feet, so it receives several feet of snow during the winter and its landscape is full of huge Ponderosa Pine trees.

Perhaps the most treacherous time to enjoy the outdoors in Sedona is during the summer. Rattlesnakes, scorpions, and cactus are a threat to people and dogs alike. Heatstroke and sunburn can sneak up on you very quickly. Thunder and lightning storms are as spectacular as they are dangerous. Most unexpected are the risks of getting lost in the vast wilderness and encountering flash floods. As the name implies, flash floods appear to come out of nowhere and have been the cause of many deaths in Northern Arizona.

Hiking Preparation

The biggest danger to hikers probably is not armed military spooks lurking in the woods. Most hikers' biggest danger is complacency. A few years ago, my wife and I were hiking on Doe Mesa where we encountered a woman unable to find the trail down to the parking lot. This woman was not wearing a sun hat and wore only yoga pants and a tank top. Despite the fact that she was only in her thirties and appeared to be in better than average shape, her lack of appropriate hiking attire, empty water bottle, and confusion bore witness to her unpreparedness. We were literally only 100 yards from the trail that led back down the mesa, yet she had been wandering for over two hours and was starting to panic when we found her. From the trailhead, it is only about a twenty-minute walk to the top of the mesa. We were up there with our dogs to have lunch, nap in the shade, and then head down. So, we filled the woman's water bottle and she followed us back down to the trailhead parking lot. Some mesas do not look that big, however if you lose your bearings, then you may find yourself wandering and lost for hours.

Similarly, a surprisingly large number of people climb up Bell Rock, even only partially, and become stuck or disoriented. The hike up Bell Rock seems easy because you can see the road and parking lot, just a stone's throw away, but hiking back down is tricky. Maybe it is the vortex energy there that gets people off kilter. The hikers who become stuck are the lucky ones; many people fall off the narrow edges, only to become seriously injured or dead.

To say nature "heals anything" is an overstatement, but getting outdoors in Sedona can be the experience of a lifetime. Sometimes just turning off your cell phone on a hike will help you get in touch with nature, your spirit, and even your primal instincts. Nature seems to have a power to rebalance people, with or without vortex phenomena. On the other hand, nature can be a heavy-handed teacher. Recently I saw a survival show in which prior contestants were offered a second opportunity to retest their extreme skills. A woman, who survived by herself for fifty-seven days in 2015, returned to the show in 2018 only to last eight days. What went wrong the second time around? Well, she did not do anything wrong or differently; she had a flare-up of multiple sclerosis, so her legs would not cooperate with her. She did not have a flare-up the first go round, even though she did have the disease. If she had never returned for that second opportunity on the show, it may have appeared as if being isolated in nature miraculously cured her.

Fortunately, the contestant used common sense by calling for rescue help on a satellite phone. Keep in mind this woman was a very well-trained professional. Imagine if you hike too far off the beaten path and have no cell phone signal. Or, even worse, imagine if a well-meaning person suggests that you head out to the forest on a "vision quest to find yourself," only to discover you are woefully unprepared for the journey. Tourists and locals alike get lost while hiking around Sedona; search and rescue operations occur frequently. Most lost hikers are often literally within a mile or two of their cars. Many thanks to our amazing fire and rescue teams for their continued daring and courageous back country helicopter and ground rescues! Make sure you proceed on your hikes with a healthy amount of caution, or else you might find yourself on a permanent trip to the "spirit world."

Running out of drinking water while hiking is a big concern; always carry more water than you think you will need. Do not rely on drinking the water from local creeks or from standing pools of water. I have come across more than one group of people being told by hiking guides that the water in creeks and pools is safe to drink because Sedona is "sacred." I have heard other guides tell people that as long as they "restructure" the water with Reiki, it will be perfectly safe to drink. One time I heard a lady explain to another hiker that she does not pick up after her dog (as Arizona law requires) because she "restructures" the dog poop molecules with Reiki, rendering it totally "safe and clean for the Sacred Land." Maybe I should have asked her to go step in it for proof.

Outdoor preparedness extends to pets. A dog off leash on hiking trails is illegal and a huge "pet peeve" for some locals. Other locals view all of outdoors as "their backyard" and disregard the leash law. I have seen coyotes sneak up behind people while walking their dogs in daylight and other dogs have been snatched by coyotes in the center of town. Likewise, sometimes coyotes jump residential backyard fences to grab dogs. Add in the danger of rattlesnakes and it seems like a no-brainer to keep Fido leashed if you love him. High summer temperatures, cactus, and foxtail grasses also pose problems for dogs. On a ninety-degree day at the Bell Rock trailhead, I saw a family walking from the trail carrying their dead pitbull. Dogs can overheat in as low as eighty-degree temperatures, and the frequently dry air dehydrates them very quickly.

Foxtails can get into a dog's skin and actually travel into their bloodstream, leading to many problems and even death. Prickly pear cactus is abundant and a dog running loose is in danger of coming home with the spines stuck in their paws, skin, or snout. Unleashed dogs also chase spirit guides relentlessly; it is a real drag.

Bell Rock Jumpers

Back when "the world was ending" on December 21, 2012, a large number of Sheriff's deputies patrolled Bell Rock to keep people away. Why? A friend informed me that up to 200 people were expected to climb

Bell Rock that night, with the idea of jumping off into a supposed portal that was to open at midnight. This same friend told me he would be in the Bell Rock parking lot that night eating popcorn.

I asked him, "Do you really want to be there watching and eating popcorn? I mean, what if some of them actually jump?"

He replied, "I didn't even think of that. I just want to see if the portal is really gonna open up."

One morning I was driving past Bell Rock just at the right time to see someone jump off Courthouse Rock, the huge formation adjacent to Bell Rock. Fortunately, this jumper was wearing a parachute and was not counting on a portal.

Oak Creek: A Real Crap Shoot

"We do not swim in your toilet; do not shit in Oak Creek" should be posted along the banks of Sedona's beautiful Oak Creek. Oak Creek can be a big problem for the unsuspecting; it is heavily polluted and literally full of shit, which causes major problems for dogs and people. Between leeching residential septic systems along the creek, storm runoff, people pooping near the creek, and diapers left in the creek, the shit level has been raised to "No Thank You." Even Joint is Always Lit will not go in and he is invincible to everything in the earthly realm.

My dog received treatment for a serious eye infection, believed by my veterinarian to have come from allowing her to swim in Oak Creek. This eye infection caused cysts to grow in her eyeballs, leading to a $1,800 eye surgery to save her sight. I have heard from a few massage therapists that patients often show up with horrible skin infections from swimming in Oak Creek. Sadly, these patients must be turned away due to the contagious nature of the infections. Waterway pollution really is a shame. I grew up on the Housatonic River in Connecticut that was heavily polluted from PCBs. As a result, I never ate a fish from it during the entire twenty-seven years I lived there.

Thinking Oak Creek is immune to harmful pollutants because it flows through "Sacred Sedona" is very naive. Oak Creek looks beautiful, but it is polluted, even more so at specific times of year. The Slide Rock Fire in May 2014 added to the problem, as the burned off vegetation increased runoff erosion. Included in the runoff were the chemical fire retardants that were dropped by helicopter to put out the fire. You would probably be safer peeing in your water bottle, like they do on those survival reality shows rather than drinking from Oak Creek. I would not recommend doing either, but that is just me.

Environmental Impacts

Anytime you see grass, it is either artificial or heavily watered. In the desert, large green lawns and lush golf courses are almost impossible to maintain, that is without the use of harsh pesticides and herbicides. Our veterinarian urged us never to take our dogs for walks on certain golf courses after hours. Due to the turf chemicals, she has treated many dogs with very bad skin problems on their foot pads.

Numerous Medicine Wheels once existed all over Sedona's wooded areas and vortex sites. Locals became pissed when the forest service dismantled them, but they were newly constructed, not historic. I personally wish the Medicine Wheels were still there, but with the large number of tourists, they would probably encourage more people to keep on building things that arguably should not be built. Along some trails, hikers create "cairns" and stacked rock formations, which definitely and rightfully chaps many people's asses, because as benign as they appear they can actually disrupt fragile ecosystems. Buddha Beach by Red Rock Crossing has become overrun with tons of these rock stacks. It is encouraged to leave rocks as they are. In the grand scheme of things, worse crimes are being committed, but it all adds up and these acts ruin the natural beauty of Sedona.

When compared to widespread environmental destruction around the world, Sedona is still in "okay" shape, but if more people, locals and tourists alike, would practice "leave no trace," then Sedona's forests may return to great shape one day. Locally, there is a sign posted on forest land that reads something akin to, "Area closed due to vegetation regrowth." That "closed area" gets about fifty head of cattle grazing on it every year. How is that for extreme irony and hypocrisy? Oh well, in regard to conservation, I would rather put a drop in the bucket than nothing at all. I would encourage all those who visit Sedona to do the same.

Wild West "Wildlife Whisperers"

In addition to not falling for ridiculously dangerous and misguided advice to drink untreated water in the Sedona wilds, use common sense against assurances that wildlife can be "reasoned" with. I have heard firsthand and read scores of online discussions from people who think that Sedona is a sacred land that causes the animals here to vibrate on a higher level of consciousness. Therefore, they believe they can openly communicate with wild animals; likewise, they believe wild animals will respond to reason. This can be dangerous. I have seen people talking to rattlesnakes to try to make them "understand" their good intentions so that they will be convinced to slither off a hiking trail. I have heard firsthand people's stories of "hiking with" packs of coyotes. Most likely, a pack of coyotes that is "hiking with you" is actually hunting you. Fortunately, my life coach is a martial arts black belt and expert coyote wrestler, so I have never had a problem with them.

On very rare occasions, you may actually have a positive experience with a wild animal that is beyond explanation. There are many stories of wild animals saving people. Recently, three wild lions supposedly saved a girl from kidnappers in Africa, which obviously is an extreme exception and not the norm. I would not try to communicate with any potentially dangerous animal in the wild; most likely, you or the animal will wind up injured or dead. Similarly, feeding wild animals and getting them too familiar to humans will usually result in them being killed. Wild animals interacting with people in a "cosmic" way is the very rare exception, not the rule.

I am probably one of the most open-minded people you will meet on this subject of animal communication who still has both feet grounded in reality and yet proceeds with extreme caution. What I have learned over the years is that if an animal is acting way out of the ordinary, it very well might be a higher power that is sending the animal as a messenger or helper. It could also be impossible to know if a mammal is a "spirit guide" or simply rabid and coming to attack you. The story of the lions saving the little girl in Africa is so extraordinary that it should be viewed with awe. It was probably divine intervention, not an experience that should be expected as commonplace. However, divine intervention is not something that can be replicated at will, especially when dealing with wild animals. If an animal chooses to let you know it is watching you, it will open the communication in a way that does NOT require you to seek it out.

Please Do Not Feed the Javelinas

However, quite often people have their minds made up about this subject, regardless of the facts. I have two neighbors with vastly different opinions about javelinas. The first time I met my new neighbor, he had just arrived in Sedona. He had been in Sedona for only a week and he wanted to eradicate every single javelina on the planet.

My other neighbor, an elderly longtime resident, had quite a different outlook. The first time I met him, I was walking my dog. He was in his garage with the door open, sitting in a recliner that faced the street. He had the garage barricaded with a wall of plywood, while twenty-five to thirty javelinas of all sizes roamed his driveway.

He was tossing them food and talking to them, "Here ya go Jenny, that a boy Dennis! Some for you Marjorie, and don't forget little Timmy."

I got out of there before the javelinas saw my dogs; they are known to attack dogs, which often results in serious injuries and death. I had a neighbor lose two huge pitbulls that tried to take on a pack. The sad irony is that the javelina-loving neighbor feeding them is the one who was responsible for the death of most of this javelina herd because his actions made them unafraid of humans. This neighbor continued feeding the javelina even after the local wildlife authorities warned him numerous times not to do so. He and three other neighbors were subsequently attacked by the javelinas as a result of his behavior. Therefore, for public safety, Arizona Fish and Game officials had no choice but to kill around twenty javelina of this herd.

Enjoy the Sedona wild lands if you get the chance; there is really nowhere else like it. Just do not become complacent out there. Mother Nature can wrap you in a big sunshine hug one minute and then kick your ass with a rattlesnake bite the next minute. Any wild animal approaching you should be considered rabid, and reptiles generally do not respond to a kind tone of voice.

    Complacency in the wilderness can have deadly consequences. Just because you watch people running around naked in the woods surviving on reality TV, does not mean that you will come home safely, even if you are fully clothed and properly equipped. What looks easy on TV is usually impossible in real life. Avoid feeding wildlife, life coaches, and spirit guides. Take only photographs; leave only footprints. Well, take a little vortex energy if you must, but keep your shorts on for God's sake and make sure to leave enough energy for the next guy's hemorrhoidal karmic disturbance.

Chapter 4

Yard Sales and Estate Sales: Windows of the Soul

Survival Tip: Always wear safety glasses to yard sales. You never know when you will be invited to an impromptu sword fight.

  The bad news is that Sedona's wild lands are off limits for collecting historic and ancient artifacts. The good news is that Sedona has a huge community of people with the pack rat as their spirit animal and their "artifacts" go on sale weekly. If you are in Sedona for a weekend, there is bound to be some yard and estate sale signs along the roadsides. If you follow them, you will find it is a surprising way to meet people and check out neighborhoods you may have otherwise never thought of driving through. In the past nine years or so, I have probably been to over 1,000 yard sales. I have met some "interesting" people and seen some things that I would definitely classify as out of the ordinary. With all the health problems I have battled the past nine years, going out to yard sales has been an unexpected way to get out of the house for a couple hours and connect with people, hear their stories, and even meet some friends.

  Since I moved here ten years ago, I have observed that Sedona has a revolving door of residents. People are always moving in and moving out. Either they are moving to another town, are elderly and moving into assisted-living facilities, or are actually passing on. Whatever the reason, there is almost never a weekend without countless yard sale and estate sale signs decorating the sides of streets, trying to lure people to take a quick detour and buy some treasure or junk. I am not joking when I tell you that some of these sales can be as exciting as an archeological expedition.

  After I became extremely sick from Lyme disease I contracted in Connecticut, I had to stop working. I was often stuck at home, bored out of my mind. One day I needed some storage containers, so I planned a shopping trip to Cottonwood. I was not up for the thirty-five minute drive to the store on my own, so I asked a friend if he wanted to take trip with me. He agreed, so I picked him up. Our plan was that I would drive to the store and he would drive back. On the way, he saw a yard sale sign, so he begged me to stop so that he could check it out. I hated yard sales or "tag sales" as they were known back east, but I reluctantly agreed. Unfortunately, Sedona has a strict policy against bringing spirit guides and life coaches to yard sales. It may sound cruel and discriminatory, but it is actually for their protection. Yard sale items may have karmic residue that needs to be cleansed with sage before it is safe.

Well, the trip to Cottonwood not only was sidetracked, it became unnecessary. I found the exact storage bins I wanted, for only pennies on the dollar! My friend found some "yard art" and old tools he wanted and we were only five minutes from home, instead of thirty-five minutes. The people hosting the sale were so friendly, eager to tell us all about the last fifteen years they enjoyed living in Sedona, and how they were ready to move back east to be with family. I spent about $4 for what I would have easily spent $50, as well as saving gas and time. I was hooked!

Not every yard sale has the exact item you are looking for, however. Often I "waste" quite a bit of time looking at used junk that is priced more than it would be if new in the store. However, I never look at it as a waste of time. I get to see back roads and neighborhoods, even the inside of houses I would never go into otherwise. Also, a yard sale is kind of like a neighborhood block party with no obligation to stay. If someone is fun to talk to, then I will often hang out and exchange stories. If someone is grouchy, then I just move along. It seems like the surplus of "stuff" for sale is from people who move here and then need to adjust to not having basements or attics. I often hear people joke that Sedona is one of the few places where you see two $40,000 cars in the driveway, roasting in the sun, while $500 worth of junk is taking up the entire garage.

Slightly Loved Yoni Eggs

I probably should have known not to pick something up unless I knew what it was, but I was brand new to Sedona and to the whole yard sale scene. When I saw a basket that said, "Slightly Loved Yoni Eggs $2 each," I made the mistake of picking one up and then asking what they were. These eggs were made of green jade, and ranged from the size of a chicken egg up to the size of a goose egg, I suppose. Each egg had a hole drilled through the center, with a black string pulled through. I thought they were huge necklaces, but not quite.

When I asked the yard sale hostess what they were, the old hippie lady replied with her eyes closed, "They are for bringing a woman into her power by strengthening her sacred space within."

I gulped, as I was now pretty sure what I was holding. She continued by explaining, "We start out wearing the larger eggs so that we can build up the strength needed to go down to much smaller sizes."

I felt relieved for a second, as I thought about that. You "wear" them, phew, they are necklaces after all. Next thing I knew she had her hand up her skirt and then pulled out a very small egg, which she held up proudly by its black cord.

"See, I have graduated to a rather small size and my yoni is rejuvenated."

I politely and carefully put the egg back into the basket, and then I thanked her for the very informative show and tell. After that, I solemnly vowed to myself that going forward I would look only with my eyes, rather than with my hands. This is now my standard "wise yard sale shopper technique." By the way, yoni means "vagina," in case you did not figure that out, or you did not yet read the glossary. This yoni egg experience was not a total loss; I was about to leave, but I went back and bought the entire basket of eggs. I figured if I gave them a good sage smudging, they would make great gifts for the neighborhood holiday party. Man, nothing makes a holiday party light up more than a basketful of slightly loved yoni eggs. Okay, that was a joke. Hopefully, they made their way to a yard art sculpture or to the recycling center.

The Titty Gun

Arizona has fairly lax gun laws, so over the years I have literally seen hundreds of guns for sale at yard sales in the Sedona area.

About nine years ago, I arrived at a yard sale that was located at the end of a dirt road in the VOC. The sale hosts were an elderly couple with a lot of stuff.

As I walked up, I heard this kind of scruffy guy ask, "Y'all got any guns for sale?"

The lady hosting the sale replied, "Sorry, all we got is our double-barreled snake gun behind the door and my titty gun, and we need both of those." The scruffy guy thanked her as he got in his truck and drove off.

Despite my better judgement and due to my curiosity I asked, "Ma'am, what exactly is a, um, the second type of gun you mentioned?"

She exclaimed, "Oh! My titty gun? Let me show you!"

Well, this lady, who was at least seventy-five years old, very ungracefully reached into her shirt and into her bra, revealing much more than I needed to see, and then pulled out this little double-barreled pistol. She flicked a lever on the side and popped out the bullets. Before I could object, she shoved the unloaded titty gun into my hands: sweat, bra lint, and all. The gun was a little .22 caliber derringer with mother-of-pearl grips and a stainless steel finish, which I suppose was to protect it from rusting while nestled in titty sweat. Anyway, this little pea shooter was surprisingly heavy; I have no idea how she kept it secured in her bra. However, I had just learned my lesson about asking too many questions. She explained to me that her husband bought it for her to protect her from "perverts and javelinas."

Her husband chimed in, "There are a lot of javelinas and perverts running around; ya never can be too careful." I did not even try to stifle my laugh and obvious discomfort as I handed the pistol back to her and went on my way.

Cannibals and Shrunken Heads

Sometimes I wish that the titty gun and yoni eggs were the craziest things I ever encountered at yard sales, however they do not come close. I have seen cannibal weapons from Fiji, taxidermy endangered species, artifacts from all over the world, shipwreck treasure, shrunken human heads, and as mentioned previously, enough guns to fill a dump truck. The real shock and awe is not so much the items, but is instead the human behavior aspect regarding one's possessions. Many people die with a ton of stuff in their homes. I do not think they even knew what they had hidden away in their closets. Other people who are moving out of town, even after being here for years, have barely enough stuff to fill up the trunk of a car. I have seen "vacation" houses that could comfortably house ten to twelve people, which are virtually unlived in. On the other hand, I have seen communal homes in which ten to fifteen people live in every available corner of the house, even under decks or in storage sheds. Sedona really hosts a diverse community.

Interacting with people while they are selling almost everything they own, or everything their relatives owned, or overflow of their collections, is very revealing. Some people will almost, or even literally, give away everything. On the other extreme, I have seen people selling the same stuff for the past nine years at inflated prices. They just pack up their junk and haul it over to their friend's yard sale across town. As previously mentioned, it makes you scratch your head when you see a car baking in the hot sun to the point of its paint peeling, while the garage is being used to store old Christmas decorations and broken exercise equipment.

Pot and Porn

Likewise, I have hosted my share of yard sales. I often collect too much junk that I cannot resist, so my wife makes me occasionally unload. Also, we have moved three times in the past ten years, which has provided good opportunities to clean out and host yard sales. At one sale, this sad-looking, sixty-something-year-old guy rode up on a little red scooter, wearing stained clothes and worn out shoes. He frowned, sighed, and offered me twelve cents for a fifty-cent item, to which I agreed. Who cares if it makes someone happy, right?

Well, a couple weeks later, I was walking my dogs when I saw scooter guy. He was outside of his $700,000 house polishing his brand new electric sports car in the driveway. His red scooter was in the third garage bay with his golf cart, and the other bay housed a brand new SUV.

My wife laughed when I told her. She replied, "Well, he is rich for a reason; he has negotiating skills!"

The only other mishap at one of my sales was when a guy in his twenties showed up and wanted to buy an old set of speakers.

He asked me, "Will you trade for some medicinal?"

I was confused. I was searching my Woo-Woo vocabulary bank and nothing rang a bell. I replied, "Say what?"

He said to me, "Ya know, 420, organic, homegrown ganja."

I felt like a fool. I was the guy who years ago could clear a two-foot bong and hold it so long that the smoke literally "disappeared." Yet, I had no idea what he was talking about. I had heard all the names: dank, homegrown, kush, Indica, Sativa, wacky-tobaccy, but never "medicinal." I just laughed and told him I did not have a use for that; instead, I would need cold, hard cash.

After my experience with scooter guy, I became a little more comfortable negotiating with people. He reminded me of a trick my uncle would use when buying a car; dress as destitute-looking as possible and then the salesperson would automatically drop the price by ten percent or so. Now when I attend yard sales, I wear the most beat-up shoes and ripped shirts I own and, as a result, I often get much better deals. My wife is often embarrassed as I leave the house, but excited when I come home with nearly free treasures. Seriously though, it is less about dressing for success and more about not being a jerk. I have had people on numerous occasions tell me to put my wallet away and they just gave me stuff for free after I told them a few jokes and we exchanged some stories.

One time I showed up at a yard sale in West Sedona and the guy was selling a cool painting that I wanted for my living room. He had it priced at $30, so I offered him $12 thinking we could meet in the middle. He directed my attention to a table around the corner and then said the best he could do was $25, plus he would "throw in" five adult movies or eight regular movies. Well, that was when I noticed a young father and his two young boys grabbing movies from the table. My Spanish is okay, so I made out something along the lines of, "You guys get two of your movies and I get two of my movies and we do not tell your mother, good?" Making a ten-year-old and an eight-year-old complicit in a secret porno score is really classy!

I then told the guy I did not need any movies and I continued checking out the painting. As the father and two sons were paying for their items, the ten-year-old showed off his bicep tattoo to the guy running the sale. The tattoo looked fake at first, but it was real, and this kid was explaining how it needed some spots filled in. The guy liked the tattoo so much he told the kid that he could pick out a free movie. Well, he went straight to the adult movie table and snagged one under his shirt, while dad was preoccupied looking at something else. The kid saw that I noticed, so he froze, ran back, and dumped the porno movie back onto the table. Wearing a goofy smile, he then grabbed an action movie off the other table. I wound up leaving empty-handed, but with a good laugh.

Fifty Shades of Sedona Yard Sales

Well, as I am writing this, I am wondering if this next story has the same two little boys in it from the aforementioned porno movie yard sale. Sedona is a smallish town, so maybe, but this time they were with mom, not dad. I was on my way home from food shopping in West Sedona at about eleven a.m. when I noticed a yard sale box pointing towards Uptown, right before Tlaquepaque (my computer was actually able to just spell-correct that), so I could not resist.

This yard sale had a lot of junk: a huge box of raw leather for leather-making, guitars, and tons of odds and ends. A knife caught my attention. It was an old, made-in-China survival knife. It was dull and rusty, but great for digging out weeds. The woman running the sale was my age, mid-thirties, wearing a loose-fitting, open-slit front "romper," no bra, and was a little too friendly. Because the knife was unpriced, she called her boyfriend to come out so he could speak with me. He came out wearing flip flops, a sarong (skirt for a man), and a man bun. He tried to sell me everything else there, including the box of leather scraps, before telling me he wanted $5 for the knife. I should add that he dumped out the contents of the huge leather box and under all the unfinished leather scraps were about fifty finished and partially-finished leather sex whips and wooden dildos, some bigger than my forearm. He tried to make me a "great deal" on the whole box of "erotic art." I explained to him that I did not even want one of these items, much less a huge collection of sex whips and dildos.

I offered him $2 for the knife, which annoyed him. He replied, "I could tell you were a cheapskate. You are just here to get something for free. Sorry, but that is just wrong in every sense. Namaste."

I think my visible furrowed brow caused him to feel a little badly, hence adding in the "Namaste" at the end. He walked away, apparently heated and embarrassed at his reaction. He walked around the corner of the sun tent they had set up, and then I overheard his girlfriend ask him what was wrong.

He told her about our conversation, to which she replied, "Oh, just take the $2 and sell it to him. You are the type of guy who would not even know what to do with a knife like that anyway."

He grunted something and stomped into the house. Stomping with his man bun, flip flops, and sarong made him look like some type of New Age Samurai cartoon character. Well, I literally began to laugh out loud, so I began walking up the driveway to my truck to save the poor guy any more embarrassment. As I turned, I stopped dead in my tracks and literally had to sit down in the driveway to try to stop hyperventilating from laughing so hard, not from the girlfriend's candid comments or the man bun temper tantrum, but from the surreal "Only in Sedona" scene that unfolded before me.

Up the driveway, two ten-year-old boys were screaming in Spanish and having a "sword fight" in the middle of the driveway while their mother was preoccupied looking at clothes hanging on a clothesline. The "swords," however, were not children's toys. Each boy had a leather sex whip in one hand and a giant wooden dildo in the other hand and they were battling it out in the middle of that Sedona driveway. The mother looked over at me sitting in the driveway hyperventilating, and she became distressed, probably thinking I was dying or something. She rushed over to me, and in Spanish began asking me what was wrong. At this point, I could not breathe, and I was laughing so hard that I was crying. I could barely see, so I just tried to point and direct her attention over to her two boys. She could not understand, so she ran down the driveway to get the woman in the romper. She ran back up the driveway with the woman and they both saw what I was laughing at. The mother ran over to the boys, spanked them on their bottoms, threw the "toys" at the woman, and then screamed at her. She called her a bitch or a whore in Spanish, maybe both; my Spanish is not that great.

Romper lady hung her head in embarrassment and then screamed down the driveway at her boyfriend, "You asshole, you told me you got rid of that stuff! Trying to sell it at my yard sale, really?"

I got up at that point and started laughing again, thinking to myself that just three minutes ago I was being lectured about the "immorality" of being a cheapskate by this guy who essentially provided the "props" for this ridiculous set of events to unfold. Then I turned around to see romper lady just standing there unsure of what to do.

No kidding, she put her hands together in front of her chest in prayer position, bowed, and said, "It was very nice meeting you. Namaste."

I dusted myself off, got in my truck, and made sure I took a mental photograph of that house, so I could Nam-a –stay-away!!!!

Twenty-Five Cent Striptease

Well, even after all of that, I continued going to yard sales here and there. Often I cannot resist those cardboard boxes tempting me on the way to or from the grocery store. One day I went up a side road to a very fancy gated community. Everything for the yard sale was set up prim and proper in one of those fancy garages with the epoxy-coated floors that sparkle in the sunlight. Well, these high-class folks were in store for a little more than they bargained for on that chilly fall morning. Placed on a table between the high-end art pieces and tasseled throw pillows were jeans marked with a sign, "twenty-five cents each." A middle-aged lady, with dyed blond hair and granny panties, held an armload of jeans while she stood in the center of the garage and looked around. Wait, how did I know she was wearing granny panties? You had to ask ...

As she stood there among twenty or so customers, I noticed her looking a little squirrely. I almost thought she was going to make a run for it and steal the jeans, but not quite. Now at twenty-five cents a pop, I think most people would figure that they should just "splurge" on the four pairs of jeans and try them on at home. If the jeans do not fit, no problem; just donate them to one of the many non-profit thrift stores in Sedona, right? Well, not this lady. In that forty-degree garage she dropped her trousers, kicked off her shoes, and then gave everyone a striptease to make sure her twenty-five cent investment paid off.

I was giggling by that point. Somehow, no one was filming it. The faces on the people there were priceless; jaws were dropping left and right.

Well, granny panties did not seem to care. She proceeded to try on all four pairs of jeans. I did not stick around to see if she bought any of them.

A couple years later I recognized "granny panties" when she showed up at my yard sale held at my parent's house. My wife, mother, and sister had clothes for sale, all for twenty-five cents each and placed onto a huge tarp laid on the ground. Unfortunately, "granny panties" was about their size!

As she gathered up an armful of pants and shirts, I got up and told her, "Lady, you are in luck. We are closing in twenty minutes and clothes are free. You just have to take them home. We do not have a changing room."

She replied, "Oh, no problem, I am not shy." Before I could tell her that I WAS shy, she began trying on shirts in my parent's driveway. I wish she earned the name "granny bra" or I wish she had a titty gun, because if she had a titty gun, then she would have needed a bra in which to carry it! No such luck. I had a topless and braless middle-aged woman trying on free shirts in my parent's driveway!

Coyotes, Witches, and Karma

Perhaps less shocking, but just as amusing, are the conversations I walk into at yard sales. I was at a sale in the Chapel neighborhood recently, where the two ladies running the sale asked me if I believed in coyotes. I thought I misheard them, so I asked them to clarify. Apparently, they were both very sure that coyotes were actually witches. They had seen the "physical form" of coyotes in daytime, but believed that at night they turned back into witches. They tried to convince me that "there is no way those sounds they hear at night could come from an animal." I replied that their theory seemed "reasonable" and wished them good luck.

About eight years ago, I met two retired hippie ladies who appeared to be selling almost everything they owned. I was only interested in a couple of items, but the younger lady felt it was necessary to explain every item in sight. She was a super-fast talker and the explanations were "informative," so I sat back and listened. The gist of her explanations was that every single item on the left side of the driveway was a past-life relic of hers. Everything on the right side of the driveway was owned by her friend in a past life.

I inquired as to why they were selling everything, to which she replied, "In order to break the karmic cycle of reincarnation and to reach Nirvana, of course."

Well, I became very interested when they started sharing details of their past lives. The older lady was a WWII soldier in a past life, and the younger lady was a Samurai Warrior and a soldier in the Napoleonic Wars. The items were apparently located and obtained through their guided intuition that allowed them to reacquire important items from their past lives.

The stories were very convincing and full of details upon details. Their yard sale boxes contained what looked like many antique relics, so I dove right in. There were old swords, knives, jackets, and all types of antique looking items. Everything was dirt cheap, so I was considering buying a couple boxes of items; I have an uncle that loves that type of stuff. Well, as I looked closer, I saw a "Made in China" stamp on one of the sword blades, a similar tag in one of the jackets, and a sticker that read the same thing on the bottom of one of the "antique clocks." I could not believe I almost fell for it; they were so convincing. I really think they believed it themselves because they were selling items for pennies on the dollar, even though they were all replicas and they spent a lot of time accumulating it all. When they asked me why I changed my mind, I told them I thought the items had "too much karma."

Box Stomping Bigfoot

All good things come to an end, kind of. Apparently, some of the people who have a crystal stuck up their Toot Chakra, also known outside of Sedona as a stick up their ass, do not seem to like the fact that people have yard sales in Sedona. For quite a few years, city employees and everyday people would go around town grabbing the yard sale advertisement boxes, then throwing them out or destroying them.

One day, I carpooled with a friend to the grocery store when we saw a middle-aged lady jump out of her car parked at a pizza restaurant. She ran towards the intersection like she was saving someone who was about to be hit by a car. In actuality, she was headed towards a yard sale box that she proceeded to attack, as if she had some past-life grudge against it. She jumped up and down on it, kicked it up the road, and then tore it to pieces with her hands. She then ran across the road at the busy intersection, without any concern for traffic, to attack the box that was on the other side of the street. My friend dropped his jaw, looked over at me, and asked, "What the heck was that all about?"

Before too long, people became very annoyed that their advertising boxes were being defaced. I met one guy whose very expensive real estate open house signs were thrown into a dumpster while he was using them for a charity yard sale. During the weekends, for several months in a row, Sedona's streets were devoid of yard sale boxes; they were being taken away minutes after being set up. Legend has it that a group of people started putting out fake boxes with no arrows because they did not want anyone actually following them. Instead, they filled these boxes with fresh dog turds. Imagine what happened when people began yanking them off the street and throwing them in their cars. Or better yet, imagine the lady who liked to stomp them to pieces! That is Sedona justice for you. I am happy to report that yard sales are again a regular occurrence, and the boxes stand proud and defiant almost every weekend.

My biggest regret in all those adventures was not having a smartphone to record the antics on video. I guess I have not learned my lesson, though. At age thirty-seven, I am probably one of the few people in the world under sixty who still carries a flip phone everywhere. Oh well, maybe I will give in and get one that takes video, should I ever find some Bigfoot tracks to motivate me to carry a video camera 24/7. I will probably get one at a yard sale one day, if I am lucky.

Chapter 5

New Age Nursery School

Survival Tip: Unattended medicine bags may attract entities or even rotten burgers.

In the spring of 2017, I began carving wood as a hobby, mostly creating little animals. At an estate sale, I saw a huge moose antler that someone had carved into an eagle. I had some antlers lying around, so from them I carved two very nice eagles. I then wanted to obtain some bigger antlers to carve some different artwork. My life coach introduced me to his aunt, June, who was selling a bunch of stuff. She had a ton of items for sale, and my eyes lit up when she mentioned she had a large collection of antlers. When I told her that I was going to carve the antlers into eagles, and that I planned to sell the carvings to benefit a local wildlife rehabilitation center, she offered me a nice deal on them.

We actually stayed in touch and became friends. She has an abundance of stories about Sedona that she has shared with me. June has lived in Sedona since the early 1990's, when she retired from teaching public school in Florida and moved to the Wild West. She is one of the few people I have met who lived in Sedona since before the tourism explosion when most of the side roads were still dirt, many of which had no bridges. Back then, you had to either wait for flooded creeks to empty out before crossing, or put your vehicle in four-wheel drive and say some prayers as you floored the gas pedal.

The most entertaining experiences she had over the course of the past twenty-eight years are the stories from working as a teacher at what she referred to as the "New Age Nursery School" that once existed in the Sedona area. At this point, I would like to note a particular cultural difference. Hard workers from the east coast who move to Sedona often have difficulties adjusting to the New Age Wild West work ethic, or lack thereof. In Sedona, it is very hard to find reliable employees. Business owners who do, should value them like water in the desert. It is common for employees to simply not show up for work, and contractors often miss appointment times or never show up at all.

One mid-morning, June arrived at her second-shift teaching position at the nursery school, only to find thirty-five children, aged two to five, being supervised solely by the secretary. The building smelled of dirty diapers and the place was in absolute chaos. When June dropped all of her belongings and rushed around to "put out fires," she yelled to the secretary, "Where the heck is everyone?"

The secretary casually replied, "Oh, no one could make it today except for you. They are all having personal problems. They decided to go off into the forest and meditate on the red rocks to rejuvenate their energy so they can come back and realize their fullest potential."

June replied, "The heck with that malarkey! Get someone in here to help me. I cannot deal with thirty-five kids on my own!"

Some days, almost everyone did show up for work including the boss, Bertha. Bertha was one of those old-school hippies who could have used warning labels on all the LSD she dropped: "Sometimes less is more." Anyway, she was "far-out groovy."

One morning, June's arch nemesis, Starlight the three-year-old nudist, was running around naked refusing to put her clothing back on. The nursery school was progressive for the 1990's, but they still had a clothing requirement. June made the mistake of letting her guard down while helping Starlight get her dress back on. Starlight gave her a kick square in the shin and then dropped to the ground in a fist-pounding temper tantrum. Bertha saw the commotion and rushed over.

"June?" she asked.

"Yesssssss?" June hissed back at Bertha as she held her shin.

Bertha reminded June, "We do not discipline the children, remember? We let them find their own way."

June snapped back and asked, "Why in the world would I not discipline a child who just kicked me in the shin?"

Bertha knelt down next to the nudist having a tantrum and began swaying back and forth, chanting and waving her arms about in the air.

She remembered June's question and replied, "They cannot be disciplined because all of their entities have not yet arrived. We have to keep the channels open while they are young so that their spirit helpers can find their way through the veil."

She then requested that June join her in clearing the aura of the nudist, still in a tantrum, so the entities would be able to see clearly. June excused herself and told Bertha she needed some ice for her shin.

A couple of days after the incident with nude Starlight and her entities, June noticed that a boy came to school with what looked like pink eye. She let Bertha know, and rather than call the boy's mother to come pick him up, Bertha rushed to her rolodex and called up "Doctor" Yellow Hawk. (A rolodex is an ancient artifact that Sedona inhabitants once used to store and organize phone numbers, long before the time of the cell phone.) Dr. Yellow Hawk arrived with a large satchel and a lot of theatrics. She pranced in wearing her brightly colored robes and scarves that danced around her as she moved.

Before we get back to the case of pink eye, I have to tell you about one of June's most interesting students, Cassidy. He was a sweet little three-year-old boy who never bothered anyone. His favorite activity was digging in the sandbox by himself. He would fill a bucket with sand and then carry it around to show everyone. He did not say much; in fact, all he ever said was, "rotten burgers, rotten burgers," referring to the sand in his little bucket.

Dr. Yellow Hawk set her huge satchel of potions, feathers, and crystals on the ground and examined the little boy with pink eye.

She immediately gasped and exclaimed, "I do not have the right medicine!"

She left her satchel unattended on the ground and went to pray in the shade under a tree. Apparently, Cassidy saw this as an opportunity to share his "rotten burgers." He brought his bucket over to her satchel and dumped all the sand inside while squealing and dancing around.

He then ran all around like a mad man screaming, "Rotten burgers! Rotten burgers!"

June did not say anything about the sand, and Dr. Yellow Hawk did not seem to notice the extra weight when she left for her car. Perhaps she did, but maybe she just assumed she gathered up some "entities."

After a few moments, the doctor rushed back in from the parking lot carrying a huge book. With the book over her head, she was running and yelling, "Is anyone breastfeeding? We need breastmilk!" She stopped in front of June, grabbed her shoulders, and looked into her eyes while slowly repeating, "Is anyone breastfeeding? We need breastmilk!"

June shrugged and replied, "God I hope not. These kids are all three and four years old."

Bertha hung up the phone and ran over exclaiming, "I just got off the phone with one of our student's mothers; she has milk!"

Dr. Yellow Hawk started tearing up and declared, "It is divine intervention from the supreme goddess! We can just flush the boy's eyes with the breastmilk and he will be cured in hours!"

After fighting her gag reflex, June interjected, "Did anyone obtain permission from the boy's parents?" (Nobody had.) "Also, what if this lady has hepatitis or AIDS or even just an infection? Have you all lost your minds?" In the end, they wound up calling the boy's mother who took him to a pediatrician.

June continued to work at the New Age nursery school for a couple more years, despite all the hiccups. She had a very high tolerance for the Woo-Woo atmosphere. Anyone who has had a toddler or has taken care of one knows that potty training time can be extremely challenging. I have never had to deal with this issue and I fortunately do not remember that time in my own life.

One especially challenging case at the nursery school was a little two-and-a-half-year old girl named Harriet who was used to being rewarded with candy for doing a "pee-pee on the potty." The nursery school had a strict no processed sugar policy, so this was quite the dilemma for little Harriet. The first time she went pee-pee on the potty she politely requested her candy. When she was informed that no candy was allowed, she went ballistic. While still seated on the bowl, she bellowed, "I want candy for my PEE-PEE!!!" She then ran through the school knocking over everything in sight. As part of the no discipline policy, she was just allowed to run herself tired.

Eventually Harriet accepted the candy-free policy, succumbed to the rule, and then became successfully potty trained. She was happy to accept a toy doll or a read-aloud story instead of candy for her pee-pee.

Many of the boys were not so easy to deal with. When the school began an outdoor garden, it became a fun place for the students to go and dig in the dirt. For some of the boys who loathed the potty, it became their favorite spot to poop.

It all started one day when the kids were digging in the dirt and the teachers were distracted weeding the garden. One of the little boys just pulled down his pants and took a dump in a hole. The other boys observed his joy that came with the freedom of pooping outside in the open, so they joined in. By the time the teachers noticed, four diapers were on the ground and as many boys were squatting in the dirt, fertilizing the garden. Due to the no discipline policy, the boys were praised for pooping like big boys and for their take-charge, maverick approach. One thing led to another, and so for the next few weeks boys were running to the garden every time they had a turd ready to come out. The trend caught on so well that eventually the garden had to be fenced off and the teachers even considered putting a litter box filled with dirt in the boy's bathroom. June did not stick around to find out. She filed her resignation and moved on to find employment elsewhere.

Chapter 6

UFOs and Aliens

Survival Tip: Make sure your tattoo artist is not a jerk.

Recently, UFO sightings have gone mainstream nationwide. Most people remember the March 13, 1997 Phoenix Lights, but there is something surreal about conservative news anchors covering UFO sightings in a serious way. In this aspect, Sedona is probably at least a few decades ahead of the rest of the country. Local news reports usually ignore UFO sightings because they are so commonplace. The local news tends to focus on out-of-the-ordinary events, usually involving groups. One of the most memorable news events in 1987 was when thousands of people gathered around Bell Rock in hopes that it would open up and reveal a spaceship that would take them all away. Spoiler alert! They did not get their spaceship.

Historically, the Sedona area has a very high rate of supposed alien abductions. Some estimates are as a high as about 34.97% of the population. There is also a very alarming rate of anal probes reported among about 99.99% of abductees. I was fortunate to be included in the lucky 0.01% who avoided an uncomfortable anal probe during my abduction experience. Just before moving to Sedona, I actually got a tattoo on my lower back that was supposed to read "Spiritual Warrior" in Sanskrit. Unfortunately, the tattoo artist was a real jerk and instead wrote, "Danger! Explosive Gas, Exit Only" in Chinese. I became very depressed for a while and thought about getting it removed with lasers. However, when I was abducted I was fully awake and to my delight, the aliens were fluent in Chinese and heeded the warning tattooed on my back. As a result, I was not probed. I am pretty sure that the tattoo artist was acting with divine purpose.

The whole phenomena of scary alien abductions and anal probes are very passé. The hip new trend is to find an alien willing to be your baby daddy or baby momma. I wish I were joking, but an entire community of people believes they have little star children on spaceships. It is rather interesting to note that some of the human-alien hybrid enthusiasts in the world are very excited about aliens creating human hybrids, but they are adamantly opposed to GMO farming. Some of them are also into promoting veganism, Non-GMOs, and organic lifestyles. So altering foods genetics is bad (to which I would agree), but combining human and alien DNA for intergalactic evolution is exciting? That is a real head scratcher.

I once received a call from a much older friend who lives in Connecticut. He is in his early fifties and is a UFO fanatic. He asked me, "Have you met this alien girl? She is a hotty and man I want to meet someone like her!"

I said to him, "You realize she and a few other young millennials are spreading their stories of how they have had amazing sex with reptile aliens, and now have intergalactic babies on spaceships as a result?"

He paused and replied, "Yeah, but she is also into organic clean living, plus she is totally hot. I mean come on!" He is still in Connecticut. Sedona has not "called" him loud enough, not yet at least. Maybe if he gets a convincing alien costume, then he could shack up with his twin flame.

I have another local friend whose wife almost secured him an alien roommate. When my good friend and his wife were looking for a roommate back in 2010, this very nice middle-aged woman showed up. My friend was at work, so his wife introduced Joint is Always Lit and me to their prospective roommate. My spirit guide and I went out to the pool; the sun was very bright, so my spirit guide and I put on sunglasses. The really wild thing is that as they exited the sliding door onto their ground-level patio, a UFO appeared in the sky above their condominium complex. Even in Sedona, daytime UFO sightings are not that common. As the two women walked towards the pool to meet us, I had an uneasy feeling; even with the intense sunlight, this lady stared at us, wide-eyed and unblinking as she shook our hands.

After we told her our names, she started talking in a kind of monotone robotic voice. "I am from the intergalactic society of light healers originating from what you would call the 13th planet in your solar system. I have a doctorate of light healing in advanced quantum phototronics and have reached the highest levels possible that I can hope to achieve in this lifetime." Then she started crouching down and turning her head from side to side as if she was trying to see up our noses. At that point, Joint is Always Lit could not stop laughing, and I was trying not to laugh either. She let us know that she was trying to see our eyes under our sunglasses. A long, awkward silence followed as Joint is Always Lit tried to stop laughing, while my friend's wife tried to look serious and not make eye contact.

Finally I blurted out, "Congratulations! When do you move in?"

She never did.

On the surface it is a funny story; on a deeper level it is very sad. Obviously, she had a couple of screws loose. After I met her, I saw her a few times hanging out at a local restaurant. She was asserting her intergalactic status in an effort to persuade people to buy her free dinners and drinks. People like that make many other people reluctant to share their UFO sightings for fear of seeming as wacky as she is. However, I have to admit I was almost surprised the UFO did not come to pick her up after the roommate situation did not work out.

Chapter 7

Bigfoot, Aliens, Marijuana, and the Cloak of Invisibility

Survival Tip: Don't Bogart that Joint!

    A big surprise for many people is that recreational marijuana is not legal in Sedona. It is remarkable how even though Sedona is in the center of Arizona, a pretty uptight state overall, many people come here and think there is a magical rainbow that connects it to California. When we lived in our condo, our neighbor was growing funny looking "tomato" plants on her patio. She was actually very appreciative and stunned when she was made aware of the aforementioned illegality of the marijuana plants she was cultivating. She got rid of them the next day.

    Some tourists told me they had been in Uptown Sedona where they happened to see a famous comedian sitting on a bench just chilling out. I will leave you guessing a little, but he had a big hit TV show back in 2003-2006. He then just kind of disappeared for a while. I had seen this guy live in concert when he came to my college, so I was intrigued. As it happened, the comedian was aware that the tourists had recognized him, so he hid his head inside his shirt.

    He proceeded to peak out the top of his shirt, then said, "Ladies, please no pictures. I will buy you an ice cream. I will hang out with you, but I am as high as a kite and I don't want any pictures on the Internet!"

    The ladies obliged, respected his wishes, and ate some ice cream on his dime while he made them all just about pee their pants with his stories and stoned antics. There are many stories about celebrities in Sedona, but that one makes me smile every time I tell it.

    A few years ago, I went to see my wife at her job in Uptown Sedona after I had just finished going to several yard sales. After I visited her, I walked back to my car, which was parked in the upper-level of a parking garage. As I walked along, I noticed an old sedan double-parked, with a guy about my age sitting on the hood of the car, finishing up a joint. He wore white-guy dreadlocks, a patchwork quilt type of shirt, camo cargo pants, and military boots. He placed his roach into the bowl of a small bong that sat on the hood next to him.

He called out to me, "Hey man, if I can get your parking spot, I'll let you have a bong hit of this dank homegrown."

I told him he was welcome to my spot, but I had not smoked in years. He looked rather disappointed. He cheered up when my spirit guide took a nice, big bong hit. It seemed as if the guy wanted to hang out for a little bit. However, he did not seem up to the challenge of parking his car. To stimulate his motivation, he lit up the bong, took a huge hit, and filled the air around him with a cloud of smoke.

"Are you in a rush? How about I tell you a story I usually do not tell people?"

It is important to know that if someone in Sedona precedes a conversation with, "I usually do not tell people," it probably means they have told at least half the town twice. Because my spirit guide was so high that he was hallucinating, I was not in a rush, and this guy seemed harmless, so I decided to sit down on the concrete wall and hear a story. His bong hit kicked in and his eyes were almost swollen shut. There is no analogy; he truly looked like he had just smoked a joint and then finished up the roach in a bong. This guy was as high as a UFO on turbo-drive, which was painful to see. He rubbed his eyes and cursed himself for losing his sunglasses. I grabbed a pair of sunglasses that I had just bought at a yard sale and gifted them to him. If anyone needed them, he did.

He started to give me a hug to thank me and I told him, "Not really my thing, just enjoy the glasses." He shrugged, started giggling, and began chasing Joint is Always Lit while trying to pet him on the head for good luck. I put an end to that very quickly and reminded him that he was going to tell me a story.

"Oh, yeah, yeah. I usually do not tell people this, but your aura was speaking to me. Last year about this time (it was early summer), I was camping up by the Bradshaw Ranch. I was by myself; I didn't even have my dog yet. (He motioned to a little Chihuahua curled up asleep on the passenger seat.) At three a.m. I woke up from these bright lights. I got out of my tent and saw that a big UFO was landing! It was only fifty feet away! I was so scared I thought I'd shit myself. Three little aliens came out of the craft and gave me messages in my brain about shape shifting, invisibility, and other cool stuff. They told me that the next day I would need to change my body and become like a Bigfoot. They said all the power was in the ganja and that I had to pay them for the knowledge. I had a few joints rolled up like always and they pointed at my shirt pocket where I had them in a cigarette box. I offered them the box and they motioned that I light one up. I sat with the three aliens and we passed the joint round and round. Man they could really handle their herb."

At that point in the story, he looked at me and asked, "You tracking with me bro?" I nodded my head and he continued. "Well, they showed me all about how to become invisible and change into other creatures and stuff. It was really easy; smoking the herb makes it a piece of cake."

I took out my flip phone, which takes pictures, and asked, "Could you change into something so I can get a selfie with you?"

He replied, "Not here, someone might see." He was so giggly at that point; I was surprised he did not end his sentence with "Silly Goose."

Well, after that, his bong hit really took over and he was on a roll. He told me all about how the spaceship took off and he went right to sleep and forgot all about it until after breakfast the next day. After he remembered, he decided to go on a hike, get high, and contemplate what it all meant. While hiking, a couple miles away from his camp, he was about to smoke a joint and meditate, when he heard a strange sound and saw a big furry creature in the distance. According to him, he smoked one of the joints immediately and turned invisible so he could get closer to the creature. At first, he thought it was a bear, but as he came within thirty yards, he could see it was a female Bigfoot.

I should mention that there is a well-known local legend of a female Bigfoot that hangs out by the Bradshaw ranch. Explanations for it being able to stay hidden usually point to interdimensional portals that it can access. Back to the story…

The Bigfoot began sniffing the air and making cooing sounds. The hippie guy was pretty sure the Bigfoot was sniffing either the marijuana smoke or him; he was not sure if invisibility masked human scent. He recalled the shapeshifting techniques the aliens taught him, so he took a big hit on the joint. As he blew out an enormous smoke cloud, he emerged as a full-grown Bigfoot, twice his normal human size and much taller than the female. The female Bigfoot looked startled at first and then relieved. She motioned to the joint he was holding and beckoned him to share.

They sat down in the forest and smoked the joint together and "talked" about a lot of "things." I do not recall what they talked about specifically, and I never asked him if she spoke English or if it was telepathy or whatnot. All I remember is that she was losing her "powers" and had been waiting for the "sacred herb" to restore her powers of invisibility. Apparently, Bigfoot has to smoke marijuana every ten years or so in order to maintain its ability to become invisible. The Bigfoot gave the pothead a special red stone as a token of her appreciation. He showed me the stone he was wearing around his neck, on a wire-wrapped necklace.

He then looked at his watch and said, "Damn! I am like three hours late. I gotta get going."

I tipped my hat to him and told him I would move my truck. As I started my truck, I looked in the rearview mirror to make sure my path was clear. His car was there, but he was gone! I looked all around and then jumped out of my truck; maybe I was experiencing a contact high, but I was expecting to see a Bigfoot, or a … I do not know what! Joint is Always Lit was no help. He was chanting messages to his home dimension in the passenger seat, mumbling about how he wanted a bag of chips and a banana split with fudge and sprinkles on top. As I continued looking all around, the pothead jumped out from behind a car, dancing with his bong in one hand and smacking his knee with the other hand.

He yelled, "I just messing with you, man! If you wanna see me invisible, we gotta meet up in the forest one day!"

I have heard a bunch of other Bigfoot stories from locals, but I think that one takes the cake, or the joint. There are stories that range from footprints, to rustling noises in the dark, to telepathic communications. I met a lady who told a story about a bunch of little furry aliens that scared some boys and caused their dog to jump off a cliff. The dog presumably died, but showed up a few days later completely healed. My life coach has heard similar stories, so it is probably true.

Very recently, I had a neighbor in the VOC report to me that she found what appeared to be Bigfoot tracks in her yard. Before telling me, she told her neighbor, who lives on a small hobby farm.

Her neighbor was not surprised. In fact, she said, "That would explain the aliens that help me to take care of this place. Bigfoot and aliens are often spotted together. They feed and water the animals and even shovel up manure for me."

She asked, "What the heck does Bigfoot have to do with your undocumented farm workers?"

She replied, "No silly, they are the UFO type of aliens. They come at night and do all my chores for me."

My intuition tells me that this story has a 77.77% chance of being true. It is Sedona after all. Stranger things have happened.

Chapter 8

Psychics, Channelers, and Mediums

Survival Tip: If you have any doubt, Nama-stay-away!

Psychics and channelers are similar, but also quite different. Psychics tend to specialize in reading thoughts, telling the future, or speaking with the deceased. Channelers usually receive lengthy messages from the afterlife, spirits, aliens, or even gods and goddesses. Mediums mostly speak or act as a conduit for deceased people who wish to communicate with the living, or vice versa. Sometimes these professionals help people find their spirit guides or guardian angels. It is almost impossible to know which psychics, channelers, or mediums are real and which are fake.

Satire Alert: I may have already mentioned that I am the most powerful psychic in the world. I know exactly what you are thinking, "Wow, this is the best book I have ever read. The author is incredibly handsome. I feel so blessed to be sharing this sacred journey with him while he holds space for me on the astral plane." I also channeled a message from your alien spirit guide, "You should lay off the marijuana brownies. You have become a little too spiritual for your own good." Wow, those were powerful messages! I know you are blown away by my abilities, but try to stay grounded.

Entire books and magazines exist in the market that claim to be 100% channeled content. In other words, the authors did not come up with the information; all they did was write down the messages they received. Some channelers perform live or they take videos of themselves while channeling. You really need to watch a channeler live, in person, to experience the full effect; some channelers speak in made-up languages, others chant and sing, and some speak English. It is remarkable that so many people take a channeled message as gospel without any proof whatsoever. Joint is Always Lit tried channeling a book to me once, but he smokes so much pot, it is very hard to get him to stay motivated to do anything.

Most people who are ripped off by psychics fall victim to scary claims of any type of "curse" that only the psychic can remedy. People have been cheated out of their life savings by believing, and giving into, the terrifying possibility of a curse that needs to be removed. The power of suggestion is a very dangerous thing. The placebo effect has proven to have a very positive impact on pain reduction and, in some cases, to cure diseases. The dark opposite would be the introduction of an illness, real or imagined, by a psychic or medical intuitive. People can experience detrimental effects to their well-being if they are convinced that they are ill just because a psychic falsely claimed that they were.

When I was nineteen and battling a few undiagnosed chronic illnesses, my naturopathic doctor on the east coast became concerned that I was not responding to treatment. She gave me the phone number of a medical intuitive and advised me to seek her opinion. If I remember correctly, the medical intuitive charged about $40 for thirty minutes. Over the phone, she was able to fairly accurately describe a few guardian angels that I saw after one of my NDEs. I was convinced she was not making up this information, since I had not spoken about it to anyone at the time. However, she was honest and said there was so much going on that she could not pinpoint a cause of my suffering. To her credit, she did not try to talk to me longer in order to get a bigger paycheck.

From what I have heard of other people's experiences with psychics, I was very lucky. That medical intuitive could have strung me along and scared me into thinking I had something incurable, or any number of possibilities. Instead, she was ethical and kept the phone call to the agreed-upon $40 for thirty minutes. I have heard countless stories of people being manipulated for months by unethical practitioners in an effort to keep the money flowing.

Since my medical intuitive consultation, I have not had any psychic readings, not even in Sedona where they are available everywhere. I have at least two friends who claim psychic abilities, but neither of them has made it a career. A friend of mine, who had considered psychic work, shared the following tidbit of information that should be of great interest to anyone considering getting a reading.

My friend went to a job interview at a venue seeking to hire psychics, in a New Age town similar to Sedona. When she arrived, she was briefly asked about her abilities and goals, but that portion of the interview literally lasted only a minute or two. No authentication tests or sample readings were required. The employer only wanted to know when she could start and if she could pay the rent. My friend was rather confused by the rent aspect, until the job was explained to her. She would be an independent contractor and could set her own hours; all she had to do was pay the significant monthly fee, well over $1,000, for the space. The monthly price depended on the size of the room. In that venue, no credentials were required; people were simply paying rent to work as psychics. An alternative route that many psychics take is to set up a website with a working phone number. I am not sure what the standard is in Sedona, but as with anything, buyers beware.

Of course, the aforementioned scenarios do not mean there are not qualified psychics who do what is expected. However, anyone with cash for rent or a website can become a psychic overnight. Just food for thought: if a psychic claims that you have cancer, a curse, or some bad karma to cleanse, then ask for some proof before you believe that you are doomed.

The "Squirrel Turd Interpreter"

As I mentioned before, I have never been to a psychic in my ten years of living in Sedona. What I did not mention is that my dog has had a psychic reading. In July of 2012, my wife and I adopted our first dog, a sixty-five pound black lab mix from the Humane Society of Sedona that we named Walks on Leash. Walks on Leash was house-trained, very obedient, and insisted on riding home on my lap the day we adopted her. Our vet told us to get her in shape because she was about fifteen pounds overweight. Since she was only eleven months old, we felt it should be easy to help her drop the extra weight with diet and exercise. We put her on a grain-free diet, took her walking every day, and brought her down to the Big Park School in the evenings to run with other dogs in the little dog park. Considering about twenty people visited the park nightly, Walks on Leash had plenty of dogs to run with, and apparently plenty of suckers, errr I mean, potential clients were available for a local pet psychic. Technically, it was not psychic reading; it was "animal interpreting."

One night, I went to the dog park only with Joint is Always Lit, since my wife was too tired to go with me. I overheard a woman telling people that their dogs were married in past lives, how they were depressed being apart, or how other dogs had anxiety from their karma. Some people greeted her by thanking her for their sessions and reporting that their dogs were "much better," but they needed another session. The psychic agreed, but indicated that it would be expensive because they were going to go "deep into the psyche." Well, when she saw my spirit guide and me for the first time, she made a beeline towards us with a business card in hand.

She could not shake our hands until she gave us her business card, because in her other hand she held some sort of wand with a huge crystal on its end, feathers tied around it, and with what appeared to be horse hair glued to its base. She introduced herself as an "animal interpreter." Joint is Always Lit and I introduced ourselves, and then my spirit guide started to introduce Walks on Leash by saying, "This is Walks on Leash. She is a black lab mix. We think she is also part golden retriever because of the purple spots on her tongue. We just rescued her from…" Before Joint is Always Lit could finish, the "interpreter" grabbed his arm and then partially closed her eyes and rolled them towards the back of her head. She pointed the crystal wand upwards to the sky and started shaking her entire body violently. Then she began talking to herself.

"Okay, yes, oh yes, I understand Walks on Leash. I will let him know." The pet psychic said to my spirit guide, "Walks on Leash is traumatized from her past and is in desperate need of a soul retrieval."

I replied, "Maybe it is lost in her backside; she is always licking it like she lost something and is trying to get it back."

The pet psychic seemed confused by my comment. When we declined further service, the lady just shrugged. She then continued to hand out business cards and give "free readings" to other dog owners.

On our way home, my spirit guide, who speaks from the other side of the veil and has at times needed an interpreter, told me he thought the lady should instead introduce herself as a "Squirrel Turd," because she was totally NUTS!

Some other people at the dog park were really on par with the animal interpreter lady. It was one of those times my spirit guide and I expected to meet some semi-normal people we could hang out with, but not quite. After meeting the animal interpreter, I met the "do you have a bag?" lady. Anytime she saw a dog dropping a deuce, she would run up to the owners, wave dog poo bags at them, and ask, "Do you have a bag?" The first time seemed reasonable since we were newcomers.

The third time she asked me, I just replied, "No, I just learned how to restructure the poop molecules with Reiki. I will just bare hand it and save the bag."

Obviously, I was joking and cannot really restructure dog poop with Reiki. On the other hand, pun intended, bare handing is one of Joint is Always Lit's special abilities. He makes jaws drop every time he scoops up soft serve chocolate pies off the ground at the dog park.

The most annoying person at the park was the guy with the horny poodles. He had two male poodles who, despite being fixed, would try to mount anything that moved. My little beagle hid under Walks on Leash, who stared and growled quietly at the amorous poodles.

Other dogs were not so lucky; instead of disciplining his horny poodles, the owner would just shout out, "Those are my sons! I taught them everything they know!"

The best dog "show" was an old golden retriever who apparently had anal gland issues. He would sit down on the top of the small grass hill and go down on his butthole as if it was a waterslide. Maybe he needed the vet to treat his anal glands, or maybe he just needed a trip to the cooling vortex to heal his hemorrhoidal karmic disturbance! In any event, I would have actually paid the $50 to hear what the animal interpreter had to say about the horny poodles and the butt slider.

Miss Mary Jane's Whispering

It should go without saying, but psychics and paranoid spouses, who smoke too much weed, do not mix well. My old buddy, Max, has a very sweet wife named Julie whose only problem is that she used to be jealous to the point of being neurotic. In addition, she loved getting high, and her almost debilitating paranoia would not keep her from her best friend, Miss Mary Jane (marijuana). When she lit up and went to a psychic for relationship advice, the Woo-Woo stars lined up for an almost perfect storm.

One day, Julie walked by the office of psychic reader, Madame Not Sure What Her Name Was. Unable to resist her impulses, Julie went inside to ask for a reading. For a $129 love donation, Julie received a surprisingly accurate reading; however, the interpretation was not exactly spot on, to say the least. Madame Not Sure What Her Name Was told Julie that she very clearly saw Max dancing with another woman, handling sexy lingerie, and watching provocative, perhaps even pornographic, material. Immediately, Mary Jane began whispering into Julie's ear, making her very paranoid, so she quickly paid the Madame and rushed home to tear the house apart to look for evidence of Max's infidelity. About all Julie found was some loose change and a couple of joints she had hidden around the apartment. She was exhausted and had the munchies, so she grabbed a bag of chips and then passed out in a food coma on the couch.

Max came home and screamed in terror as he walked through the front door and saw the house torn apart and his wife passed out on the couch. He thought they had been robbed and his poor wife beaten unconscious. Upon hearing Max's screams, Julie woke up and became a bit embarrassed at what she had done to the house while high. She reluctantly told Max everything about her psychic reading, including her dramatic search of the entire house for evidence to prove the psychic correct. Max just closed his eyes, grabbed Julie by the hand, and walked her out to the driveway. He handed her the keys to his car and told her to open the trunk.

Julie was sure the trunk would contain all the evidence she needed to say, "I told you so!" Instead, she saw a gift-wrapped box, with an attached card addressed to her. Inside, the box contained lingerie items, all in Julie's size and favorite colors, along with an instructional couple's massage DVD... not exactly porn.

Julie looked confused and blurted out, "Yeah, but what about the other woman? Explain that one!"

Max walked Julie back inside. He turned on the music player to their first-dance song from their wedding ten years ago. Max explained that he had been taking dance lessons so he could dance with Julie; she had always given him a hard time that he danced at their wedding with two left feet.

    Anyway, good thing Julie had a couple of joints left. According to Max, he smoked at least one and a half, and then went to bed early while Julie put the house back together. Overall, I guess the psychic was kind of right?

Chapter 9

Is Practicing Yoga Cultural Appropriation?

Survival Tip: Avoid the head and tail of the dragon, and maybe the entire body, too.

Recently, some Social Justice Warriors and college professors have expressed concerns that rich white ladies practicing yoga is cultural appropriation. Considering that yoga was brought to the USA by yoga practitioners with the express purpose to spread knowledge, health, and enlightenment to Western culture, the accusations may be a bit heavy handed. However, it is very true that most of the yoga taught in modern studios is a far cry from ancient and more traditional yoga practices. For personal safety, I would be concerned about "masters" who are teaching some dangerous and misleading techniques. For example, I have been to yoga classes where ladies in their sixties, who have never practiced any yoga, are encouraged to do unassisted headstands.

Furry Teacher

Years ago, Joint is Always Lit and my life coach regularly forced me to attend yoga classes in the VOC. The female yoga instructor wore long sleeves and yoga pants to the first three or four classes. After the same students attended regularly, I guess the instructor became more comfortable; she began wearing sports bras and shorts to teach her classes. Not a big deal, except she had more leg hair than most men, and enough armpit hair to house a few baby birds! The furry teacher flashing her armpit bushes was prophetic in a way, because the following week she was ill and had a substitute fill in, who had a bit of an armpit fetish. The sub was more of a qigong teacher, so her entire class focused on self-love and stimulatory body tapping. For forty-five minutes, we stood around tapping and patting our bodies in a rhythmic sequence. Additionally, each body part had a corresponding affirmation chant; when we began tapping our armpits the chant was, "I love my armpit, I love my armpit, I love my armpit…"

One time, my grandmother came to watch the yoga class. Afterward, she told the teacher she loved how she taught and wanted to know where she was from. I overheard the teacher tell her, "I am from Venus. This is my third time on this earth plane."

On the ride home my grandmother asked me, "How much do these yoga teachers make?"

I told her, "I do not know, but probably about $40 an hour."

She then asked, "How the heck does she fly from Phoenix to Sedona three times a week?"

It took me a little while to explain that it was not that type of plane, and that she claimed she was from Venus, not Phoenix.

My grandmother's response was something along the lines of, "You know this and you still think it is a good idea at the end of class to lie on the floor with your eyes closed in corpse pose while this nut job watches?" I simply reminded her I was protected; Joint is Always Lit was watching over me.

Farting Baby

Well, the yoga teacher was not the only one who became very comfortable after several classes. A fellow student, an older lady, liked to drink a little wine before class and a whole lot afterwards, but unfortunately it gave her gas. When it was time for us to perform yoga rolls, she would bust out machine gun style farts. At first, she tried to hide it by coughing, but if you have ever tried to cough and fart at the same time, you know that does not work. So there she was rolling, coughing, and farting away. It sounded something like, "Cough, cough, fart, fart, fart. Cough, fart, cough, cough, fart, fart." My life coach has a really juvenile sense of humor and just loved it.

During the next class, she did not even wait until the yoga rolls to begin farting. She blasted farts during "happy baby pose" and instead of coughing to conceal the noise, she proudly declared, "That was me!"

The teacher closed her eyes and proclaimed, "That is okay. That is the magical power of yoga. Namaste."

The wine often caught up with the farting baby by the end of each class. Every session concluded with silent meditation in corpse pose, during which farting baby would instantly pass out and disrupt the silence with her chainsaw snoring.

Golden Drinks: Not Just for Survivalists

Years ago, I met a yoga "master" in Sedona who sold yoga merchandise at a swap meet near Posse Ground Park. Last I heard, he was living in a cave in another state and teaching yoga. I am not talking about your conventional "downtown hip studio style yoga." On the contrary, he was teaching people how to drink urine and even bathe in it in order to achieve ultimate health and longevity. This guy has received quite a bit of attention; however, this practice is really not new. I asked my life coach to teach me the practice, but he is a real germophobe and therefore refused.

Urine drinking is a very ancient practice in which devotees traditionally drink their first pee of the morning. It is important to avoid the "head and tail of the dragon," which is the very beginning and end of the flow. The reasoning is that there is more likely to be contaminants and bacteria at the beginning and the end of urine flows. After twenty years of drinking my own urine, I can report ... NOT! I cannot even claim that I ever snuck a little taste; I am not that brave. Furthermore, from a Traditional Chinese Medicine view on drinking urine and semen, partakers who ingest these bodily fluids are essentially recycling used hormones and chi. Some tantric practitioners advocate drinking semen if it is discharged, while others say it is a mistake to do so and you will not recover the energy that is lost during orgasm. It seems like either practice is similar to taking hormone replacement supplements and medications; over time, consuming these replacement hormones cause the body to stop creating hormones naturally. So, besides the "ick-factor" of ingesting urine or semen, one might instead significantly alter the body's ability to produce its own hormones when these bodily fluids are consumed regularly. If that is too complex for you, think of it as similar to smoking the resin out of a marijuana pipe.

I have a feeling that many of the people "teaching" others how to consume their own bodily fluids are doing it simply for the shock value. Yoga is big business and yoga studios are a dime a dozen. What is not yet commonplace are pee-pee drinking classes. Maybe I am wrong; perhaps urine smoothies will one day bring us a new golden age in Sedona. Joint is Always Lit can see the future and actually knows the answer, but he is forbidden from sharing that sacred knowledge.

Chapter 10

Gluten-free Cultural Appropriation

Survival Tip: Gluten-free brownies will probably not align your chakras.

In some instances, such as in Native American artwork and ceremony exploitation, Cultural Appropriation is harmful and can hurt minority populations. In other instances, it is just a way to feign outrage over hairstyles or clothing choices. Along these lines, the New Age culture has birthed an annoying monster, known as the gluten-free lifestyle, which has resulted in the appropriation of celiac disease. As someone with celiac disease who has seen all the crazy disinformation surrounding the gluten-free phenomena, I think some information may be of use to people caught in the gluten-free web of confusion. Unlike similar fads, it does not seem to be a passing trend. It has actually grown exponentially in the past decade, especially in health-conscious areas like Sedona.

Celiac disease is an autoimmune disease (in the same category as lupus and multiple sclerosis) that only affects one percent of the general population. It causes the body's immune system to attack the small intestine, which results in malnutrition, vitamin and mineral deficiencies, and even neurological problems such as neuropathy. Most importantly, the only treatment for celiac disease is 100% avoidance of gluten, wheat, rye, and barley; no prescription drugs or surgical treatments exist to treat celiac disease.

Years ago, my life coach worked with a lady who would buy gluten-free brownies and claimed they would "raise her awareness and bring her good karma." She adhered to a "strict gluten-free diet" until someone had a birthday. When the cake showed up, she would devour a piece of it right away. I have seen people frustrate wait staff by obsessing that their main dish be 100% gluten-free and dairy-free, only to order a brownie with ice cream for dessert. Compound this with celebrities' gluten-free wedding cakes and weight loss programs, and it seems like just another annoying "my shit don't stink diet." I actually "get it" when wait staff, cooks, and restaurant managers get frustrated with all the gluten-free hype. Many people are simply exploiting the diet as a way to claim superiority over others. Despite popular Woo-Woo ideology, a gluten-free diet will not make your poop smell like sunshine and your farts smell like rainbows.

Gluten-free food is a huge fad trending in Sedona and in the New Age movement. Sharing food with others is such an intricate part of socializing; it bewilders me why anyone would intentionally commit social suicide if they do not have to do so. That might seem like an extreme statement, but people with celiac disease cannot easily eat out in restaurants or in social situations. Sedona has many restaurants that offer gluten-free options; an item might be gluten-free, but how careful was the preparation to ensure no cross contamination? Because of this, I do not eat out anymore. For me and for many others with celiac disease, it is better to eat at home and be safe. Now, if you are on the gluten-free bandwagon just to be trendy, then by all means try one of the many gluten-free items available in restaurants. Local bakeries offer gluten-free goodies, and grocery stores have increased their gluten-free product selection over the past ten years.

Celiac and Explosions

Perhaps the most memorable instance I ever witnessed of the audible and smelly celiac disease side effects was when a teacher ignored the 504 plan of a young boy with celiac disease. She was annoyed with monitoring his dietary restrictions, so at a first grade holiday party she allowed him to eat anything he wanted. Not even thirty minutes later, the room had to be evacuated because of this kid's fart attacks. One of this boy's side effects with celiac disease was extreme farts whenever he ingested anything with gluten. He had no idea why he was having that reaction, but he thought it was great. What were not great were his long-lasting symptoms, including a severe headache, that was triggered when he ingested gluten at the holiday party. Perhaps, like so many other people, the teacher had the misconception that celiac disease is just a "digestive disorder," based on annoying "trendy gluten-free lifestyle" marketing.

My life coach and spirit guide both have celiac disease. My life coach was in good health, but his doctor finally tested him for celiac disease when he developed symptoms of extreme fatigue and "noisy" side effects. The most comical side effect was best illustrated during a family trip to the Grand Canyon. At one point during the trip, we arrived at the southeastern rim to check out the watchtower. My life coach indicated that something was not feeling right as he exited the car and walked towards the canyon. Lo and behold, his innards had built up a couple more sonic boom farts. At the watchtower, a college-age guy and his girlfriend stood about fifty feet behind my life coach and me. As my life coach blasted away, they heard it loud and clear all the way behind us. The young man laughed, yelled, clapped his hands over his head, and cheered my life coach on as his girlfriend covered her face and giggled.

That was just the opening act. The main event happened as we arrived at the top of the stairs in that little watchtower. About ten people were up there, not counting my life coach, my wife, my parents, or myself. My wife was standing next to my life coach when suddenly he blasted probably the loudest fart of his entire life. The only saving grace was that it, and all the aforementioned farts, were very loud and strike fear in the hearts of the timid, but thankfully do not stink up a room.

Other tourists started stifling laughs and looking embarrassed after my life coach turned to my wife and asked her, "Is your stomach bothering you again?" God bless that poor wife of mine for not smacking him! Fortunately, the gluten-free diet relieves most celiac patients of their explosive farts. Ever since my life coach adopted a necessary gluten-free diet, he has successfully quieted down.

Moral of this story: If you get out here to Sedona, be sure to check out the watchtower on the southeastern rim of the Grand Canyon. Not only does it have a great view, it has really great acoustics as well! On that fateful day, my life coach deserved the name Thunder Flatuence.

Gluten-Free Marketing

So, why have gluten-free products exploded in the New Age health food marketplace? Money is, of course, the short answer. Gluten-free products have become big moneymakers. Additionally, some people enjoy getting the sympathy of having a serious autoimmune disease without actually suffering any of the consequences. After all, celiac is a very serious disease; left untreated, a myriad of problems occur, including nervous system complications and neuropathy, which can be debilitating. Someone who proclaims, "I am gluten intolerant!" automatically gives themselves victim status. With so many "victims" in the marketplace, a huge demand exists for gluten-free products.

As long as people continue to view the gluten-free lifestyle as a super hip and trendy New Age health consciousness movement, then people with celiac disease will continue to suffer the consequences of the negative social stigma. Five million people with celiac disease will continue to be viewed as entitled, spoiled, obsessive-compulsive "dieters," who want to make the lives of those around them difficult and uncomfortable. Demanding 100% gluten-free food from restaurants, friends, and relatives in the absence of diagnosed celiac disease or gluten intolerance is really nothing more than a cry for attention.

Take it from me, being 100% gluten-free sucks. Eating out is impossible and trying to explain to strangers, friends, and even family why "their food is not good enough" (as they interpret it) is a horrible experience. If you sincerely believe you have an actual problem with consuming gluten or other problematic foods, then please find a good doctor who will test for all food allergies. Likewise, maybe see how you feel with a ninety-five percent reduction of wheat and dairy. If you do not have celiac disease, then you will not have to imprison yourself in a gluten-free bubble for your entire life. Most people would not demand a handicapped license plate for a sprained ankle, so why hijack, or appropriate, a disease in order to be trendy?

As fate would have it, my spirit guide and life coach also have celiac disease. We are forming a 501(c)(3) non-profit New Age Healing Group. All of the proceeds will go to a friend of ours named Johnny Marijuana Seed, who travels all over the world with a bag of marijuana seeds. He plants the seeds everywhere he goes, bringing peace, happiness, and the munchies to all far-off lands. My non-profit New Age Healing Group does not really have anything to do with celiac disease, but charity is super spiritual.

Chapter 11

Vegans, Colonics, and the "Toothless Wonder"

Survival Tip: The best part of waking up is coffee, but in Sedona it may not be in your cup.

  My life coach experimented with the vegan lifestyle after it was explained to him by a New Ager that humans who eat meat acquire karma that allows carnivorous aliens to eat them in return. While he was on this 100% plant-based diet, he began having dreams that aliens in the shape of carnivorous Venus flytrap plants were devouring him. He then decided to switch to a 100% human breast milk diet, with the idea that human-derived products are non-animal, and their karma allows them to be considered vegan. With patience, he found some people selling breast milk online. Unfortunately, his nightmares continued and he felt ensnared in a perilous booby trap. He then switched to drinking urine to sustain his life, but the nightmares that ensued were much too disturbing to share. Finally, my life coach became a Breatharian, subsisting on a diet of air alone, and he was sure he had corrected his karma. All was well, until he had nightmares that the wind was either blowing him away or surrounding him in methane fart gas, in order for it to get its karmic revenge. He gave up and now eats mostly fast food. He figures if he were going to hell, he would like to at least enjoy the ride.

  Sedona is one of the few places in the world where organic, vegan, gluten-free, and paleo diet food is as easy, if not easier, to find than fast food. Vegetarianism, veganism, and healthy living in general have been strongly associated with the New Age movement for decades. Consequently, the growing populations of health-conscious locals and tourists have increased the demand for healthy foods and local entrepreneurs have listened. Furthermore, alternative approaches to wellness are prevalent in Sedona; many healing modalities are easily available, including colon hydrotherapy and coffee enemas. Some of these therapies can be a one-stop, one-day procedure at a day spa, or they can span to several days or weeks at a wellness retreat center.

I will concede that from all the research I have done regarding veganism, it is probably one of the healthiest diets available. However, there is a big caveat; it needs to be done correctly. In addition, associated juice fasts and colon cleanses have shown potential in some people to be life changing. The key word here is "some." Like anything else, a qualified doctor should be consulted before taking any drastic measures with your diet.

Too often, the overall message of health and environmental well-being really gets lost in the weeds. Before I moved to Sedona, one of my college professors was a self-proclaimed "vegan warrior." He was hardly your run-of-the-mill progressive, vegan hippie. During every class, without fail, he would make all of us squeamish as he paused class with a hand gesture; he would close his eyes and then rip out some of the loudest farts ever.

Each time he would exclaim, "Oh Toothless Wonder, what message do you have for us today? We praise your words of wisdom! Feel free to impart any knowledge upon us as you see fit!"

He seemed to consider his vegan warrior quest more about what came out of his body than what he put in it. He would have fit in very well with the student in the yoga class I mentioned earlier.

Vegan Fluids and Facials

One day I was in Uptown, picking up a pizza for my dad. Considering I had not eaten a "real" pizza in about nine years, I was probably drooling a small puddle onto the pizzeria floor. As I stood there waiting, I could not help but overhear a young woman with purple hair and her friend talking on a bench behind me. They were agreeing with each other that they would both confront their partners. There would be no more oral sex unless their partners agreed to be 100% vegan. They formed a pact that they could not ingest, in good conscious, the sperm of toxic meat eaters any longer. I was thinking, "Only in Sedona," as my appetite quickly left me. Well, apparently not "Only in Sedona," many articles in trendy magazines address this very topic, which has become quite the moral dilemma for many vegans when evaluating potential romantic partners. Tragically, this exact issue is what ended my life coach's last romantic relationship.

As synchronicity usually flows so smoothly in Sedona, I was ready for anything as the day progressed. As fate would have it, someone on that very afternoon posted a similarly themed article on a Sedona social media page that piqued my interest. It was about a nice young lady who has become famous, or at least infamous, by her online posts in which she documents her entire "vegan experience." Well that is not out of the ordinary; millions of vegans post online. However, she is unique in that she incorporates semen smoothies and semen facial care into her vegan lifestyle. I guess the only reason I was shocked was that she was not from Sedona. Somehow, even though she strongly maintains that she is in no way involved in the extraction process, she has a friend who supplies her with daily doses of sperm. Apparently, she claims that she needs the daily "gift" to realize her full energetic potential. With stories like this, is it any wonder why many people cannot take vegans seriously? Joint is Always Lit has informed me that a propensity towards veganism has to do with being a marijuana plant in a past life; that karmic residue will follow you into your next life.

Colonics and Coffee

If you have a friend who gets a colonic, good luck trying not to hear details about it. My wife and I had friends who went for a "couples colonic." Of course, since we were in Sedona, they apparently thought their "his and hers" colonics would be excellent dinnertime conversation. I just remember the petite, hundred-pound, five-foot tall wife turning bright red when her husband told us, "Man, for such a little thing, was she ever full of shit. You should have seen what came out of her!" I lost my appetite. Thank God he had not taken pictures on his phone!

Less invasive, but maybe as wild as a colonic, is the "big cleanse," which could be referred to as the "big dump." These cleanses initially became popular when manufacturers of psyllium husk laxatives spread urban legends that certain celebrities "died with forty pounds of impacted fecal matter in their colons." Anyone who has had a colonoscopy knows this to be complete nonsense. Psyllium husk will make you take gigantic dumps because it sticks together in your bowels like a big blob of glue and therefore gives the deception of colon cleansing. If you pour psyllium husk in your drain, it will clog it severely.

Another very interesting, lesser-known practice is the coffee enema. Commonly used during fasts and juice cleanses, users claim that coffee enemas supposedly detoxify the liver, stimulate the liver and gallbladder to release waste, decrease depression, increase mental clarity, clean the colon, and may even act as a pain management technique. Best part of waking up, is coffee in your butt!

I have read many sources that claim your body cannot absorb the caffeine from a coffee enema. Well, I had considered believing that at face value, even though I never tried it, until I saw a new trend on the news. The trend was not exactly vegan related; it was more college party related. Of course, I am talking about "butt-chugging," infamously known as "boofing." Do not like the taste of beer? No problem; let your buddies stick a tube in your butt attached to a funnel and you can just butt-chug it. This may sound comical, but it is actually very dangerous. My life coach lost control of his rectum for three months due to boofing, and Joint is Always Lit actually lost a good friend to the practice.

I was intrigued, not because I planned on butt chugging, but because of the related claims about coffee enemas. Considering that the alcohol in beer is clearly absorbed and kids were getting very sick, then it would be plausible that the caffeine in a coffee enema is absorbed as well. It seems that the sources I was reading about coffee enemas were fibbing; they were trying to sell people on extended fasting programs and did not want to scare people away with caffeine absorption. They should have just been honest. Caffeine is absorbed, but at about 3.5 times less than if orally administered.

Just Breathe ... But Do Not Drink Bleach

Who knows if any of these therapies are actually effective forms of healing. When I worked for a veterinarian in high school, we often made house calls to dairy farms. One farmer had an outbreak of diarrhea among his cows; he proudly boasted that he stopped the spread of the illness by pouring some bleach down the cows' throats. I still remember the look that vet gave me when the farmer turned his back. A bleach smoothie was the farmer's form of "alternative healing." He really thought it was helping his cows, but he was lucky he did not kill them. Joint is Always Lit knows the farmer's spirit guide; he is a real jerk.

    If you cannot afford organic, gluten-free, or vegan food, then what can you do? The answer is to just breathe. In past years, this concept called Breatharianism has gained popularity in Sedona and in the New Age culture. Literally, this latest "diet plan" consists of absorbing all of your dietary needs from the air you breathe, or even from the energy around you. Some of these Breatharians make a big production out of it. They swallow air and may even loudly burp afterwards, simulating that they are very full and satisfied with their "meal." That does not seem to jive with what ancient texts and traditional practitioners say about this practice. It would appear that they have simply accomplished the goal of convincing others that they survive on air alone.

    As with anything New Age, some folks will try to take things to the extreme after reading some ancient text that sparks their interest. A woman in the grocery store the other day was reading off bar codes to the cashier because she "could not tolerate lasers contacting her food." I overheard another girl who was adamant that she could not loan out her water bottles anymore, not because of germ phobia, but because her friends were choking on the crystals that she placed in the bottom of all her bottles to restructure the water.

    Joint is Always Lit tells me we are all worried about our health and the environment for no reason. He has channeled the cure for global warming to the most important world leaders, which is actually common knowledge among the cosmos: On November 11, 2011, everyone in the world who was over twenty-one had to light up a really fat joint and ask the universe, or aliens, or maybe both, to heal the hole in the ozone. It may alarm you that we missed the deadline. Do not worry. Joint is Always Lit informed me that a cosmic portal will open up when politicians cease talking out of their arses. At that point, we will be able to jump timelines to an alternate universe where unicorns not only exist, they also crap sunshine and fart rainbows. Oh yeah, on that timeline aliens or the universe or whatever already healed the ozone.

Chapter 12

Making Friends in Sedona is Hard to Do

Survival Tip: Lightsabers and bong hits do not mix well.

If you have a pickup truck, a guest house, or even a free "crash couch," then you will probably manifest and attract an abundance of new friends quickly. Many people in Sedona are nomadic couch surfers who are constantly moving. Some of the yoga retreat teacher types set up home bases in Sedona and travel all over the world to teach. Unfortunately, many, many friends of mine have moved out of Sedona, mostly due to the high cost of living.

Two different couples, who my wife and I were friends with, moved to Costa Rica, one after the other. The first couple made a business deal with a Sedona local to run a Costa Rican yoga retreat center. The couple sold everything they owned and relocated, but after they arrived in Costa Rica, they unfortunately discovered the deal was not what the man had promised. The other couple that left Sedona had businesses in other states prior to moving here. They moved to Sedona in hopes of opening another business, but the startup and operating prices were just too high for them to get their foot in the door. Business rental spaces in Sedona are ridiculously expensive, so it was much more economical for them to move to Costa Rica.

Early in my Sedona residency, I became good friends with a man named Tuktovam, who was a descendant of Noah, yes, THAT Noah ... from the Bible. He had lived in Sedona with his son for a long time, maybe too long. Tuktovam was still married, but his wife, Asheemara, went to live in an ashram in Texas to reevaluate her life purpose. A few months before we met, she caught him practicing tantra with a neighbor. Asheemara took it as a sign from the goddess that she might need to find a new spirit path.

God bless Tuktovam. Aside from his New Age infidelity, he was a great guy, but holy guacamole; it was an adventure every time we got together. After he lost his house to foreclosure, I volunteered to help him move to a rental house. Did I mention I have a pickup truck? He had to move again one year later when the landlord decided to convert the house into a short-term rental, so I offered to help him with a moving sale. He wanted to sell everything that did not fit in his hatchback and move to Texas.

At this point, I should back up to his Christmas party, which took place a few months before his move. My wife was exhausted, so she told me to go to Tuktovam's party with my life coach. We arrived around seven in the evening to a lovely after-dinner party: tons of Christmas cookies graced the kitchen counter, a warm fire blazed in the fireplace, and rats scurried all around the house. Yup, Tuktovam's three pet rats had escaped from the guest bathroom's bathtub, where they lived. His two large dogs were chasing them around the living room, but ironically, the six cats were not at all interested in the chase.

Eventually his son caught the rats and brought them back to the bathroom. During all the commotion, two of the cats jumped onto the counter and stepped on the cookie trays. My friend did not seem at all concerned; the cats were allowed to just do their own thing. I forgot to mention that in his former house he shared a bedroom with his son. They rented the other room to a lady who had a pet snake, which was a real point of contention. The roommate bought the rats as food for her snake, but my friend rescued them from her in exchange for buying frozen rats for her snake's meal. In addition to the two large dogs, three rats, and six cats, Tuktovam and his son also owned two free-range indoor rabbits, which were likewise problematic. Rabbits cannot be litter trained, so they just placed sheets over the beds and couch and then let the rabbits poop and pee all over the place. Nighttime was a bit more civilized; the rabbits slept in the closet on a fresh bed of hay in a dog crate.

After the cats stepped all over the cookies, my life coach and I both politely declined them. We asked for a drink instead. Drinks were served in old glass tomato sauce jars; he also owned regular glasses, so I guess repurposing old jars was a new trend. When I had to go to the restroom, my friend accompanied me to the door. He had to make sure I got in and out, but also that the rats stayed inside. I was advised that I might wish to pee sitting down, not because he thought I would pee all over the floor, although that is what I initially thought. The advice was due to the propensity of the rats to jump in the toilet for a swim every time the seat went up. They could only be trained to stay clear of the toilet when someone was sitting on it. Tuktovam offered no guarantees with someone standing in front of it.

When I was done in the bathroom, two other guests, a mutual friend and her husband, finally arrived. They were late because they decided to walk the half mile to the party and they were both already shit-faced. Yet, my friend's husband was there for only two minutes and he already had a tomato jar in his hand filled with vodka and orange juice.

The evening was rather uneventful after that. The drunken guy took off his sweater and played bongos on his beer belly. In Sedona, that is nothing out of the ordinary. They were so drunk; they left after forty-five minutes because his wife was worried about the walk home in the dark. Forget the walk home; he made it to the end of the driveway and then fell face-first into the drainage ditch. That was not funny! What was funny was that he was so drunk; it took about five minutes and everyone's help to get him out and onto his feet.

Tuktovam was working seven days a week to save enough money for his move to Texas, therefore I volunteered to run his moving sale so he would not miss work. I had no idea what I was in for; Tuktovam had enough stuff to fill a two-car garage to the ceiling. He instructed me that his yard sale was a free-for-all, and the only rule was to "make an offer" on everything. I had not been to his house since Christmas and it looked as if a group of rock stars from the 1970's broke in and partied there for a week straight.

This state of affairs did not scare people away. I sold everything, including the tomato sauce jars! One guy showed up asking for twin beds; I knew some were in the guest bedroom, but I had not yet been in there. He followed me and unfortunately I had forgotten about the rabbits that were hopping around. Little rabbit turds and hay littered the carpet. Accompanying the turds and hay on the floor was an ancient, half-eaten ice cream carton. Apparently, the ice cream had melted, tipped over, and hardened into the carpet. This mummified mess was topped off with a spoon that was cemented into the dried ice cream pool. Fortunately, the guy did not even bat an eye. He offered $200 for the set and they were sold. Well, the carpet in this house really took a beating, as further evidenced by the sale of the aquarium. After it sold, the aquarium's stand left an off-white, cream-colored "footprint" on the carpet; the remainder of the great room's carpet was stained a light mocha brown.

When it was time to see my friend and his son off, their departure was like launching a little Noah's Ark. Two suitcases were strapped to the roof of his hatchback; inside, the back seats were down to make room for two dogs, seven cats, and two rabbits. The rats and guinea pigs were reluctantly given away since Tuktovam's landlord in Texas only allowed two dogs. I guess he figured he could hide the seven cats and two rabbits, but rats and guinea pigs might overdo it. Did you notice they had an extra cat since Christmas? That is because his son saved his allowance and did not give up pestering his dad until he was allowed to spend it on another cat. "But Daaaaaaaaaaaaaaaad, I want another cat!" In all seriousness, I was very sad to see them go; they were a lot of fun. At least they never got high and attacked me with lightsabers …let me explain:

After The Ark hit the road, my wife and I were running low on local friends. Everyone we knew had moved out of Sedona, so we were very lonely. One day, we were shopping in Cottonwood where we met a nice young couple from the VOC. They were both timeshare salespeople, but we gave them a chance anyhow; after all, I sold timeshare for a few months. They invited us over one night to play some games and hang out. I thought they meant cards or a trivia game, but not quite.

When we arrived at their house we noticed it smelled very nice, like someone had just smoked some high-quality herb. The guy was playing video games while his wife was making drinks in the kitchen. We sat down on the sectional couch and I noticed a lightsaber shrine.

The night started nicely. We sat in the living room, had drinks, and talked; it was all very casual. Then the bong came out, along with the Jedi mind tricks. They offered us some weed, but we declined because I had not smoked in years and neither had my wife.

The young woman took a little baby hit, coughed a few times and then exclaimed, "Daaaaaaaaaamn! That's some good stuff." When it was her husband's turn, he did not hold back.

He took a monster hit and exclaimed, "Let's go outside and have a lightsaber war!"

His wife thought it was a good idea. We followed them as they rushed over to the lightsaber shrine where he bent down on one knee and said some type of Jedi prayer or something. His wife explained to us that she surprised him with this set for Christmas. I looked up these Jedi items on the Internet after we came home; the cost of just one piece was over $200! My friend then carefully removed a lightsaber from the shrine and then motioned for me to take the other one, which caught me off guard because I thought he was going to fight his wife. I started to decline and then I looked over at my wife, who was finally smiling with some new friends. I decided to take one for the team, so I picked up the lightsaber and followed him outside.

I thought he was going to have his wife take a funny video to post on social media or something, but not even close; he wanted a battle. This guy was about five inches shorter than me, out of shape, and had never taken a martial arts class. I could have dropped him like a hot potato, but I did not want to be a bad guest. So, I had a sword battle with him. I pretended as if I hurt my arm, and then we all went back inside. Next time they called us for an invitation to their house, I declined and then I apologized to my wife; I just could not do it again.

Holy shit, sometimes I really wish I were making this stuff up.

Chapter 13

Sedona Social Media

Survival Tip: It is a small town; communicate online as if you are talking to an alien from another planet with a bad temper, because in Sedona you just might be.

Anyone living in or visiting Sedona should check out the local social media groups. With thousands of opinionated people online in a town like Sedona, what could possibly go wrong? The locals here are serious about social media. You cannot beat it for the latest updates on traffic, restaurant deals, business promotions, and public service announcements. As negative as social media can be, I have met many very nice locals through the Sedona group pages. My life coach often goes online just to troll people and argue about politics. He can be a real pain in the ass. He is currently working with a Shaman to cure his "asstrollogy" addiction, which is the cause of his trolling and arguing. Through social media groups, I have seen many pets reunited with owners, money raised for charity events, and people posting expensive lost and found items, including cash.

On the other hand, people can be rather opinionated when it comes to "Sacred Sedona" issues, so buckle up for those social media posts. An example was a couple of years ago with the Sedona/Verde Valley Red Rock National Monument proposal, which was an attempt to designate nearly the entire Verde Valley a National Monument. It was a big source of contention among residents because so many people live in the area and had the proposal succeeded, then Sedona would have become the only city to be enclosed inside of a federally run National Monument.

When the proposal failed, the push to over-promote tourism to the area continued. The non-profit Chamber of Commerce receives approximately two million dollars of taxpayers' money annually to market Sedona to tourists. With Route 179 and Route 89A being the only roads in and out of Sedona, traffic has changed the city's personality. The future holds the promise of increased spending, taxes, traffic, tourism, and development. The small-town feel is becoming a memory and there is sure to be continued strife as we move forward.

On a much lighter note, I think the best post I ever read on a Sedona social media page was by a local lady who fooled many readers into believing a Bigfoot hoax that she created. She had a little action figure of a bear or something and posted a very blurry picture she took of it, along with some tracks in the mud. People were going wild arguing about whether the tracks were from a bear or a Bigfoot. One online viewer was a local "expert" who inquired about interviewing her regarding her "encounter." I just got some popcorn and watched the comments for a day or two, until she began posting clearer pictures, revealing it was just a plastic toy. Lack of perspective is one of the side effects of viewing the world through a three-inch cell phone screen. The other is opening up your Inbox to a bunch of unwanted dick pics. I caught Joint is Always Lit trying to send a few one time, so I channeled a message to his wife and sent him back to the spirit world for a couple weeks. He received some Reiki sessions which totally cured his sex addiction.

I have seen just about everything advertised locally online: channeling, soul retrieval, belly rub massage (for people, not dogs), and almost anything else you can imagine. The two that take the cake have to be armpit hair braiding and anal bleaching. I did not even know either of those were a "thing."

Sedona, The Chemtrail Capital

Chemtrails are the big white cloud-like streams that come out of flying planes. Sedona seems to be "the" hotspot, or at least "a" hotspot, for them. I am including them in this chapter because people are always posting chemtrail pictures and weather forecasts online. No one really knows who is responsible for chemtrails or what they are. The three main theories are:

1 – They are visually masking daytime UFO travel.
2 – They are used for weather manipulation.
3 – They contain any number of toxic chemicals and viruses that are aimed at population control or "dumbing people down."

Many "experts" in the field seem very proficient at copying and pasting information supporting their chemtrail theories. Quite a few local folks feel strongly enough about chemtrails to justify wearing surgical masks or staying indoors to protect themselves from the chemtrail spraying. However, neither I, nor anyone else, know if there is actually anything to them. Like politics, chemtrail discussions often end up in heated conversations or intense confrontations. I heard about two men who engaged in an argument about chemtrails on a local Sedona social media page. They recognized each other at the grocery store one day and a bad fight ensued, all because of those pesky chemtrails. They should have just asked my spirit guide. According to him, they are just the cosmic trails from unicorns who ride on top of airplanes to protect them from aliens, duh! If the unicorns did not leave cosmic trails, they could not find their way home.

Love it or hate it, social media is here to stay. As a result, there are no more local secrets; likewise, not many secret places remain in Sedona. The drive to one of my favorite spots, the Shaman's Cave or Robber's Roost, is on a long and rough road, but it is only about a fifteen-minute walk from the trailhead parking lot. Joint is Always Lit used to take me up there during his out-of-body experiences. I stopped going after the last time, though. He got so high that I had to walk back home. Just freaking ridiculous!

When I was a child, my dad would take my sister and me, along with our friends, to play in the neighborhood playground. One cold winter day, we were sliding down the covered slide and we all noticed that we smelled very bad after a while. Apparently, some jackass had decided to pee inside the slide and because the slide was covered, it dried up and the rain was not able to clean it! The same jackass and his buddies must have followed me to Sedona; the last time I was out at Shaman's Cave, its walls were stained and smelled like piss. I know what you are thinking, no, it was not Joint is Always Lit. He knows my life coach would kick his ass; the guy is a total tree hugger.

The beauty of being in the open-air cave is protection from the elements. The downfall is the same as the aforementioned covered slide; the cave is covered, so the rain does not clean it. The cave made the local news at the end of September 2018 when vandals painted elaborate and offensive graffiti on the walls. Profane words and pictures were drawn all over the walls with black latex paint. Someone actually hiked all the way up there with a brush and a can of paint. I sent Joint is Always Lit up there to clean it off, but his energy was too weak to complete the job. Thankfully, we have some amazing local volunteers who cleaned the environmental eyesore within days of its discovery.

    It is easy to go online to complain, start a fight, or whatever people do best when they are drunk, high, or bored. Other than bad traffic and people messing up the forest, we do not really have a lot to complain about. There has been some crime in Sedona and in the neighboring towns since I have moved here. Murders, rapes, drugs, police shootouts, and robberies are not foreign to modern-day Sedona. Social media has done a service that the local media has failed to do, and that is to inform the public. Transparency was an issue prior to the social media explosion. Tourist towns are like businesses, universities, and religious institutions that do their best to avoid bad publicity. Social media gets a thumbs-up for facilitating the Great Awakening.

Chapter 14

New Age Politics

Survival Tip: Before you point your finger, make sure your wife ain't your cousin.

      Sedona has a way of making even the annoying aspects of life, like politics, seem supernatural. I recently had an interesting conversation with a young couple in a grocery store parking lot. They had convinced themselves that they were in an "alternate universe" where Oprah became president after Donald Trump and Hillary Clinton dropped out of the race. The "real world," however, is a bit more complicated. In the past few years, the Sedona community has become divided over the issues of National Monument Status and tourism. This chapter will not get back into those topics. Instead, this chapter will simply document some wacky mishaps and run-ins, with the underlying theme of politics, which I have had in Sedona over the years. Before I start, I would like to introduce the "CTCO Mantra," which stands for "Chill-The-Chakra-Out." It is a much-needed mantra in our current climate where people on both sides of the aisle are losing sight of humanity due to politics.
      Remember way back, like four years ago, when people could talk about, or even joke about, politics without starting a war with one another? After the 9/11 attacks, it seemed as though everyone in the country was very friendly and cooperative. Even the extreme right and extreme left conspiracy theorists were getting along; both extreme groups believed it was an inside job. What the heck happened? This may be the first time in history where politics are more important to people than friends, family, and even religion. President Obama was called the Messiah and President Trump is worshipped as a god by at least one guy in India, who even built him a shrine. Why did everyone go so nutty so quickly?
      I think my late grandmother prophesied all this over-the-top craziness back in 2005 or so. I visited her one weekend when I was in college. My grandfather had passed away a few years prior and she lived alone. I remember waking up before her one morning, just in time to see her come rushing out of her bedroom to turn on the TV. When I inquired

what the hurry was all about, she replied, "I want to see if anyone shot that George W. Bush, or maybe he had a heart attack or something!" Apparently, this was a daily ritual for her. I did not particularly care for "W," but I never reached her level of disgust for any politician. I don't think most people reached her level, back then at least. Presently however, I bet half the country is performing my grandmother's morning ritual and probably the other half would be doing it if the election went the other way.

When I first met my Brazilian, Portuguese-speaking wife, I thought I would impress her by speaking her native language. The problem was that I thought she spoke Spanish. When I did my best to give her a compliment in Spanish, she did not have a meltdown or accuse me of being racist, foolish, or whatever.

She simply joked and asked me, "Didn't you pay attention in geography class? We speak Portuguese in Brazil!"

It was very ironic considering that I minored in geography in college. We have not stopped laughing at each other's mishaps since then. I think everyone would be a lot happier if we would just CTCO and laugh together.

If you really want to go to an alternate dimension, try DVR recording the mainstream left wing and right wing cable news channels. Switch back and forth every ten minutes from one channel to the other. I assure you a vortex portal will open up to another dimension; you will seriously feel like you are travelling from one interdimensional "reality" to another. People who are somewhat balanced can easily spot the divisive nature of the beast. Sadly, however, too often people find it very difficult to find any type of balance.

Joint is Always Lit is a Trump supporter and my life coach is a Bernie Sanders nut. My spirit guide was part of the crew that built the veil, which is the metaphysical wall that President Trump built in a past life to stop spiritual travelers from traveling to the astral plane. Joint is Always Lit informed me that the spirit world never wound up paying for the veil; the people of earth became stuck with the bill.

My life coach, on the other hand, is all about free Reiki for everyone and open travel between earth and the spirit world. You can just imagine the awkwardness of a sacred gong ceremony at my house.

Conversations become a little heated in our soul talks while we congregate under our copper pyramid. When Mercury is in retrograde, Nama-stay-away from my life coach and spirit guide.

Aliens of a Different Sort

As I mentioned, my wife is a Brazilian-born, U.S. and Brazilian citizen, with a lovely Portuguese accent. Since the 2016 election, she has been asked by four different tourist customers in the Sedona retail shop where she works, "Are you an illegal alien?" The first time this happened, she came home very sad. She told the customer she was from Brazil and that she was a U.S. citizen. I asked her if the customer was with a woman, which he was. I told her, if it happens again, just ask the customer, "Is she your wife or girlfriend?" When he replies "wife," ask him, "Before she was your wife, was she your sister or your cousin?" That cheered her up and made her laugh, but she is too polite to say that to a customer. Fortunately, her coworker Louise was not!

So my wife told Louise, an adamant Trump supporter, what I suggested and she volunteered to ask the "cousin or sister question" if it happened again. Despite supporting President Trump, Louise was disgusted to hear what had happened. As "Sedona Karma" would have it, this happened three more times. Each time someone asked my wife, "Are you an illegal alien?" Louise quickly turned the tables on them, asking the "cousin or sister question!" If I remember correctly, two of the three were actually cousins before they became wives and the other one was not previously related to her current husband. I am not that good at math, but I think that story determines that two thirds of racists are married to their cousins. That calculates out to about ninety-five percent, according to my spirit guide.

I am not sure what the customers were hoping to learn. Maybe they thought it would be "exotic" to meet an illegal alien in Arizona. Maybe they wanted to post on social media after they called ICE. In any event, Louise gave them much more than they bargained for!

During my first year living in Sedona, I was employed as an English as a Second Language teacher to about thirty children, aged eight to ten. A couple months into the school year, an ICE raid was conducted in the community. For three days, only five kids showed up for school. After the raids were over, I was down to about twenty-three students. The ones who remained told stories of hiding out in relatives' closets and watching movies on portable DVD players. It was quite a shock considering I had never really heard of anything like that prior to moving to Sedona. It was also very sad. Without warning, I had lost a good portion of my students and I was concerned for their wellbeing.

The parents, for the most part, were amazing. They respected teachers and they all showed up for parent-teacher conferences. The school translator was late for one of the conferences, so I had an older brother of one of my students translating for me. I was telling the parents some bad news; their son was really slacking off and not doing his homework or paying attention in class. I was surprised when they both smiled proudly and shook my hand across the table. Turns out that the older brother made everything up and, rather than translate, he was falsely singing his younger brother's praises!

Hairless in Sedona

After I fell ill from Lyme disease and had to stop teaching, I kind of gave up on fashion. I started wearing sweatpants everywhere and shaving my head to about 1/16th of an inch, in an almost bald, Buddha-style look. This "hairstyle" was quite different for me, especially considering that I had long hair in my early twenties, which I cut and donated to Locks of Love.

My wife stated when we first moved here, "Isn't it great, you can pretty much wear whatever you want and no one cares!" That was true and so was the fact that anywhere else, a white guy with a buzz cut would probably have been viewed as a skinhead or something, but not in Sedona. The day after I shaved my head for the first time, one of my neighbors stopped me outside my house and exclaimed, "I love your haircut. It is really Buddha Zen, man. I dig it!"

The next day I was at the grocery store. The cashier, a lady in her fifties, saw my haircut, squealed, jumped up and down, and asked, "Oh, can I please rub your head for good luck?" I thought she was joking, so I bent forward and said, "Sure." She was not joking and she seemed to want a lot of luck. She really got a good rub in, a two-handed rub, if I remember correctly. At least she was respectful and did not try to rub the heads of my life coach and spirit guide. She assured me that she would split her lottery winnings with me if I brought her good luck. That is how Sedona was nine years ago.

Trumped-Up Theories

Things do get strange in Sedona with all its New Age influence. As soon as President Trump announced the Space Force project, the Woo-Woos came out in full force with "I told you so" proclamations of an imminent alien attack. Attempts are made among some fringe New Agers to rationalize and explain the "spiritual meaning" of the Trump presidency. I have heard everything from Trump being a reincarnated chaotic catalyst for disruption, to a Pleiadian alien-human hybrid sent to earth to battle the Reptilian Overlord race. Some were claiming that "Trump-Pence" were the "Trumpets" from the end times as described in the Bible's book of Revelation. In any event, New Agers have become very imaginative in spiritualizing everything, including the controversial Trump presidency.

On a similar note, my wife's former coworker Louise, the Trump supporter, and not at all a New Ager, was convinced that President Trump and Hillary Clinton were holograms. According to her theory, they would send holographic versions of themselves when giving speeches and making public appearances. She had a very detailed conversation with me one day about how she was absolutely positive that President Trump and Hillary Clinton were in fact never really "there" at speeches. They were both "too smart and careful" to risk going out in public. Instead, they sent holograms to their TV appearances and speaking events. That is Sedona for ya.

She may not be that far off, though. I recently read a hit-piece about a self-helper who sold out a speaking event, but who literally "showed up" as a hologram, rather than in person. That, however, seemed more like a matter of convenience, as opposed to a safety maneuver. Very interesting theories come out of Sedona.

Chapter 15

Do You Wish to Become a Sedona Transplant?

Survival Tip: Cleanse your crystals often, clear your aura, and find your center. Red Rock Fever is contagious.

If you wish to move to Sedona and you have hopes of finding a super diverse community, with a small-town feel, where neighbors all know each other, kids play in the streets on quiet backroads, and everyone leaves their doors unlocked, then you probably will not find it. You would need a time machine to take you back about twenty years or so. There are still places like that in outlying communities, but that ship sailed a long time ago for "Sedona Proper." However, it is still a community like no other. The red rock views will be here long after we are all gone, but this town will never go back to "the way it was."

Neighborhoods, Home Styles, and Landscaping

Sedona neighborhood styles range from cookie-cutter condominiums and townhouses to sprawling ranches and hobby farms. A few areas allow mobile homes, and there's a handful of fifty-five and over communities throughout the city. Some neighborhoods, but not many, are zoned for almost whatever you want, including farm animals. Many communities have very strict homeowner association rules, along with very strict people who enforce those rules. Affordable housing is almost non-existent, unless you are considering renting a tee-pee, yurt, or even a storage shed in someone's backyard.

As far as landscaping is concerned, desert and drought-tolerant plants are not very diverse and options are limited. Just make sure that you obtain a good-sized chunk of rose quartz crystal for each side of your front door; they are essential for removing negative energy before you or your guests enter your home. If you have gravel landscaping, which is common in Sedona, don't be shocked if you sometimes find random cars parked on your yard; tourist and transplant drivers cannot always tell the difference between a driveway and a front yard.

During our second summer in Sedona, my sister drove my mom and me to weekend yard sales for some family bonding. My mom and I just about lost it when my sister parked her car right in the middle of someone's gravel front yard. Back east if you see gravel, it is most likely a driveway or a parking lot, but not in Sedona. You really cannot blame her; her spirit guide should have warned her.

Utilities

Depending on where you live, you may have to forego high-speed Internet service and good cell phone reception. I have an old flip phone because the antenna is superior to the new phones. Still, I only get a signal in one corner of my house. A very slow and unreliable Internet connection came only by satellite until very recently, when my neighborhood finally received a good and reliable Wi-Fi alternative.

Traffic, Driving, and Off-Roading

At present, Arizona is the only state to allow ATVs, off-road motorcycles, dirt bikes, and even golf carts on roadways with posted speed limits of 35mph or less. The speed limit on most Sedona streets is 35 mph, so it is common to see these vehicles driven on local roads. Many years ago, only a few small companies in West Sedona rented out UTVs/ATVs; nowadays with so many tourists, this town is overrun with them. At one point, instead of owning two cars, we owned one car and a side-by-side UTV, a two-person ATV, which was able to go almost anywhere a horse would go. This vehicle setup lasted about a year; it was a wonderful time for us to explore Sedona's off-road areas extensively.

Outside of Phoenix and Tucson, Arizona has very lenient emission requirements; as a result, many old cars and trucks in Sedona look and smell as if they are exhaling huge amounts of pollution. If you value fresh air and you are considering moving here, then you may want to buy a house located away from major streets.

A unique part of visiting Sedona is that you may have a super spiritual experience, specifically a NDE, before you even get out of your car. The bright idea to put Suicide Circles (also known as traffic roundabouts) at almost every intersection along Route 179 from The Village of Oak Creek to Uptown Sedona has created havoc. Locals have figured out how to drive through them, for the most part, but many tourists either fly right through them without yielding, or they stop in the center, causing very unsafe situations. Also, the large number of retired elderly residents on the road adds to the problem. When my late grandmother lived at a retirement home in Sedona, I saw many of her neighbors, who were legally blind and barely able to walk without a walker, get into vehicles and drive on the road. I cannot count the number of times people have nearly driven right into me at the roundabouts and how often I have witnessed other drivers have near misses or crashes. The bike lanes, medians, and turning lanes seem to be impossible to understand for many drivers. I wish they were isolated incidents, but I have seen a lot of people drive the wrong way down roads on the opposite side of a median, turn the wrong direction into Suicide Circles, and even drive right over medians. So, if you are looking for a super spiritual NDE, then you are in luck if you drive in Sedona.

Nightlife and Activities

The search for nightlife in Sedona is a fool's errand. After nine p.m. you will find your entertainment options very limited. Once a month a few full moon drum circles take place around town. There is karaoke here and there, and some bars stay open late, but pickings are slim. An attempt was made years ago to have regular live music events at the outdoor Cultural Park across from Red Rock High School, but plans fell through and that venue has gone unused. A few family-friendly events occasionally happen in Sedona; however, most events and activities consist of yoga and various physical fitness classes. Also, many free or low-cost metaphysical and tourist-centric classes frequently occur, which are often moneymaking bait for the event holders selling expensive items or future classes.

Economic Demographics

Keep in mind that however progressive, open-minded, and flamboyant some of the locals are, Sedona is located in the center of a conservative and, some even might say, uptight state. Due to various nationwide economic trends, the local demographic is quickly changing, so Sedona will never have the diversity it once did. If things keep changing the way they have been, then retirees and short-term renters will most likely be the only two groups remaining. I have not even seen a dolphin person in years.

These changes will make for a rather problematic demographic if you do not fit into either of those two categories and you wish to move here. The tension between the haves and the have nots has become very intense the past few years, and the inability to put the genie back in the bottle has many locals nervous about the future. Primarily, it is becoming very expensive to live in this town, which means that in several years only wealthy people will be able to move here. My family and I were lucky enough to move out of our condos and into houses when the housing market fell. There are many philanthropists and very admirable people in the upper economic echelons; however, I have certainly run across quite a few grouchy rich people in Sedona. Money does not seem to have the ability to dislodge the grouch crystal from the Toot Chakra.

Sadly, a large homeless population, of over one hundred and fifty, exists in and around Sedona. Some of the homeless are long-term campers and couch surfers who work, but cannot afford a residence. A sizeable homeless encampment was recently dismantled near the Sedona Airport, just outside Sunset Park. The camp was a fifteen-by-fifteen foot cave dug out of the side of the mesa, with a hidden door and interior wooden support beams. Digging and building this cave was no easy feat. Sedona dirt is like concrete and very hard to excavate. The homeless population is growing, and there is no local homeless shelter. It is a desperate situation for many, especially with winter temperatures that often fall well below freezing. On a positive note, Sedona locals recently set up several donation boxes around town that collect hats, gloves, and scarfs to help those in need.

Snobby Folks

    About six years ago, my wife received some free high-end dining loyalty vouchers from work, as a reward for her referring customers to a very expensive restaurant on Oak Creek. That dining experience let us see how the other half lives. Entrée prices began around $79 and went up from there and that was about six years ago. We saved up enough money to cover the tip and tax, which was not included in the vouchers, and invited my parents and my late grandmother, who was ninety-one at the time, to dinner. It was lovely sitting under huge shade trees on the edge of the creek, with ducks flying by and swimming in the water a few feet away from us. My mother and I have celiac disease and my wife has several food allergies, so we were not the easiest group to handle, but we tried to be very clear and patient with the waitress, who was very accommodating. On the other hand, a party of six sat behind us and, oh my, they were rowdy.

    Maybe rowdy is the wrong term; perhaps entitled snobs would better describe them. One lady sent her meal back because she did not like the "presentation." According to her, it really was not going to take a nice picture for her online blog. Another lady wanted her champagne transferred to another glass to hopefully reduce the bubble content. The husbands of the group were fairly quiet until one of them knocked his potato onto the ground. He claimed it was "precariously and carelessly" placed too close to the edge of his plate and he wanted his entrée removed from the bill. The last straw for my grandmother was when one of the ladies screamed at the waitress because she spilled champagne. No, the waitress did not spill it. The lady spilled it on herself, but apparently the waitress did not notice and did not help her dry off immediately, maybe because she was waiting on another table. Well, my grandmother had enough; we thought she was going to the restroom as she quietly got up.

    She walked over to the table and bent over close to them. I am not sure why she bent over; she talked loud enough so everyone could hear her.

    She said, "You should be absolutely ashamed of yourselves. This poor girl, who is doing an excellent job waiting on everybody, deserves an apology and a very generous tip. If I were you, I would go home wondering whether or not she spits in your dessert. I would not blame her if she does!"

The reaction from the brats was like watching a bunch of scared kindergarten students who were just told they would be sitting in the principal's office for recess. My grandmother quietly shuffled back over to the table and sat down as our food arrived. She was a character and full of energy, generosity, and love for animals. She volunteered at the local animal rescue thrift store until she was ninety-four.

More About My Late Grandmother, My Favorite Transplant

When my family first arrived in Sedona, we were all unfamiliar with the complexity of the town. My grandmother moved with us from Connecticut and experienced instant culture shock. She quietly asked my mother one day, "Did you know that this was such a wacky place when you moved us here?" In an effort to expand my grandmother's horizons, I gave her a Feng Shui book to read while we unpacked her belongings and set up her apartment. After about ten minutes, she had a disgusted look on her face.

When I asked her what was wrong she replied, "I don't know who the heck this Feng Shooey guy thinks he is! He is telling people how they should rearrange their whole life because of what he thinks. I mean, look at this! He is trying to tell people how to set up their toilets to create harmony. What an idiot!"

Apparently, I should have explained to her that Feng Shui is a practice, not the name of a New Age author. As a side note, my wife read the same book and concluded that her practice of Feng Shui was to make me get rid of everything she did not like, or to make me put it in my man cave.

I also gave my grandmother a book on crystals to read while I took a swim and she sat poolside. She read it with great intent. Her mind was sharp and she definitely had her opinions of things. After an hour of reading, she started telling me which crystals were needed for certain aliments or health benefits. The conclusion she eventually came to was that the crystal salespeople just invented all these uses in order to sell a lot of stones. In time, she joined the crowd when some of her friends gifted her crystals for her apartment.

More About Snobby Folks, My Least Favorite Transplants

It does seem like people really can become spoiled in this town. I mean, if you cannot have a good time eating dinner next to the creek, hanging out with wild ducks, you are probably doomed. About a year after my grandmother passed away, I was in the grocery store where I witnessed an irritable customer in front of me in the checkout line. She was a pudgy middle-aged lady, wearing a gold watch and designer clothes that looked like they belonged to someone twenty pounds lighter. Maybe it was the added weight of her heavy purse that made her grouchy, or the fact that her clothes were pinching her chub-chub rolls in all the right places, but money was not buying this lady any decency. She plopped down a big opened package of steak onto the checkout counter and demanded a refund. I recognized the cashier and her coworker bagging groceries, since they had been working there for as long as I had been living in Sedona. The cashier was my mother's age and the bagger was my age and both were always super friendly. Well, this lady who was returning the meat ironically looked like a sausage that was stuffed way too tightly and apparently thought that the cashiers were the CEOs of the store. The cashier agreed to give her a refund, assuring her it was not a problem.

That was not enough; the lady wanted to put on a show. She barked, "This is such an inconvenience! I have never had as many problems with meat as I have had with this grocery store!"

The lady would not shut up. She kept giving the employees advice on how they should change the store, hire better help, you name it. At that point, among all the chaos, I noticed the label on the package of meat. Against my better judgement, I pointed out some vital information.

I said, "Ma'am, did you notice that your meat package actually has the prior name of the grocery store on it, and the date is from three years ago?"

Perhaps she was on a time traveling light ship for the past three years downloading universal knowledge from the astral plane. That theory actually seems more reasonable than the reality of the situation I witnessed. Apparently, the woman did not even realize that her arch nemesis had actually changed owners and had gone through a major renovation. It was somewhat scary; the store was literally completely redesigned, expanded, and had a new name and sign out front. The cashier politely informed her that the store was renamed over a year ago. At that point, the customer's face became so red that I became nervous; I was worried she was going to give herself a heart attack and I might have to do mouth-to-mouth on this old grouch. I then remembered the new CPR guidelines: no mouth-to-mouth breaths, just chest compressions … phew!

Well, of course the lady apologized, right? Not at all. Instead, she exclaimed, "Well, if the store would stop changing names, then things would be less confusing. At least I got my refund after all this fuss!"

Then it was my turn to check out. The two employees, despite the previous debacle, had the courage to ask me, "Was your shopping experience okay? Did you have any problems?" To my extreme delight, the grouchy lady was fumbling with her purse at the end of the counter and was well within earshot.

I blurted out in a very loud and obnoxious tone, making sure the sausage lady could hear, "I bought some ice cream here two years ago and it was too cold!!! Do you know anything about storing ice cream? I should be able to buy ice cream and have it be the perfect temperature! If you had any sense you would make sure that when people buy ice cream it is not too cold!"

At first, the cashier and bagger looked like proverbial deer in the headlights, probably thinking, "Here we go again!" Then they saw me grinning and looking at the end of the counter. The stuffed sausage lady picked up my sarcasm immediately.

Wow, if her face was red the first time, this time I thought her head was going to explode. She stormed out of the store without looking back. The checkout ladies were giggling at that point and as I left one of them whispered, "Thank you." Keep in mind, there is a good chance that this entitled and confused richy-rich designer stuffed sausage, with the three-year-old meat and the extremely bad attitude, might be your neighbor if you move to Sedona. On the other hand, unfortunately, the cashier told me a year ago she had to move because Sedona was becoming too expensive. Last I heard, the lady bagging groceries, who obviously has a good sense of humor and a lot of patience, was on her way out, too.

Unless you have a very high-paying job lined up and enough money saved to buy a house, it will be very difficult for a single person, or even a couple, to afford a stable long-term house rental in Sedona, based on the low local wages. Many people who work in Sedona live outside of Sedona, as far away as Cottonwood, and have a forty-five minute work commute. Short-term rentals are spreading all over the Verde Valley and soon it may be impossible for working class people to move to and live in the area. Keep this in mind if you have a spirit guide or life coach to feed: the cost of living is ridiculous and is increasing.

If, after reading all of these wonderful stories in this book, you still want to cure your Red Rock Fever by leaving it all behind and moving to Sedona, then you must be a very brave person. You must also be brave enough to push past the dire warnings of "the ancients." They warned us that Sedona was not a place to be lived in. So, I wonder, were all the cliff dwellings just timeshare vacation caves? The remnants of elaborate irrigation systems, farmland, and other signs of permanent community settlements, suggest otherwise. The folklore that suggests Sedona should not be inhabited is a contemporary idea, not an historic one. There is a shared mentality among many Sedona transplants that they should be "the last ones in." In other words, Sedona's door was open for them, but they slammed it shut and it is now closed for you and anyone else who wants to follow. A word of caution: The rush to move here can be quite tragic; many spirit guides are left behind in the process. Just about every week in Sedona, a soul retrieval retreat is held so that people can reunite with their spirit guides that they lost during their mad dashes to the red rocks.

Chapter 16

Thinking of Running a Business in Sedona?

Survival Tip: If people introduce themselves as light workers, it does not mean they do not work hard. They do not work lightly; they work with the light. In fact they may be the light; it just depends on their auras.

Opening and operating a business in Sedona will continue to be increasingly challenging as time goes by. Commercial rental rates are skyrocketing. I have heard absurd numbers, but I would rather not try to make a best guess average because I may be way below what is actually the present norm. The positive aspect of running a business in this town is the sheer number of tourists that frequent the area, providing your business would benefit from tourist traffic. However, the number of visitors is not consistent throughout the year; tourism declines sharply in the winter and summer, and many employers either reduce work hours or lay off employees during off-season months. If you add in the job insecurity and the lack of affordable housing opportunities, you create the perfect storm for a severely depleted employee pool.

It is not uncommon for jobs to go unfilled for very long stretches. Many business owners wind up having to work extra hours to perform jobs they would much rather hire someone else to do. If you plan on coming to Sedona and simply buying or opening a business while you sit back and observe from a distance, then you might be in for a rude awakening. The number of small businesses that have opened and closed in the past ten years is high enough to make most people nervous. The number of businesses that are still open and in the same location as they were ten years ago is relatively low. Many investors seem to be using the short-term rental house business model as the moneymaking opportunity of choice.

Problems with Employees

If you were to view a fast forward video clip of a day's worth of Sedona job interviews, it would not be unusual to feel like you were watching a bad montage of a Woo-Woo dating site. The most brazen job interviewee I ever heard of was a psychic who specialized in Feng Shui. She was not interested in the regular job at all. Instead, she wanted the store owners to pay her $777 so she could tell them where to place crystals in order to attract more customers and make more sales. It might sound ridiculous, but my life coach actually made a living doing that for years before the 2008 recession hit the economy.

The stories I have heard from business owners about employee mishaps in Sedona are out of this world, but not in a good way. Keep in mind that many of your employees, coworkers, and neighbors may be somewhere on the Woo-Woo spectrum; so failure to show up for work, or being very late, are a given. In my wife's home country of Brazil, it is not uncommon for employees to take time off work every four years to watch the World Cup. In Sedona, it is not uncommon for employees to take time off work every time their "energy is off" or when the planets are in retrograde. Meditating on the job is as commonplace as neglecting customers while playing on a smartphone. Employees who fear receiving bad karma can also be problematic. I knew a retail store owner in Uptown who had an employee redirecting customers to their competitor's store where prices were lower on certain items. When confronted, the employee told the owner that "she did not want the karma of allowing the customer to pay more money for the same product."

I made the mistake of recommending a longtime friend of mine, Skeeter, for a job at friend's store in the Sedona area. I visited him at work one day expecting to find him busy getting the new business up and running. I became a little jealous. My friend was outside making many new friends without me. He was feeding old bread to a squirrel while "communicating" with a hummingbird in the tree. He was excited to tell me that the hummingbird was slowing down time for him so he could enjoy the moment with the squirrel. I raised my eyebrows, concerned I had not made a good recommendation.

Skeeter may have lacked worth ethic, but his customer service skills were top-notch. He would bake brownies and bring them to work on the weekend when the store was very busy. He informed me that when someone made a big purchase or seemed to be in a bad mood, he would offer them a brownie. I understood the reasoning behind rewarding a customer for making a big purchase, but not for rewarding a bad mood.

When I asked Skeeter about his lopsided reward system, he laughed and replied, "These are my special good-mood brownies. I add in some St. John's Wort extract for depression and some marijuana butter for good measure. I make the butter myself and it always puts me in a good mood." The customer is always right and the customer is always high.

Fortunately, and perhaps unsurprisingly, none of the customers ever complained. However, I think the brownies may have explained Skeeter's extracurricular animal meetings. On a positive note, nothing ever went missing or was stolen from the store. However, my friend finally wound up being fired after he left the safe wide open at the end of the day on three separate occasions. Moral of the story: if you find good help in Sedona, do your best to keep them!

The employee pool has recently become even shallower; in fact, a few large businesses had to stop new employee and routine drug testing because almost everyone was on something and they would not have employees left had they continued testing. A business owner I know received a call in the fall of 2018 from a lady inquiring about work.

The lady boasted, "I have been clean for thirty days and I haven't even stole nothing lately."

Alternate Business Models

If you do come up with a successful business model and find reliable employees, you may not be able to implement it, at least not legally. For example, it is illegal to guide tourists without a proper permit, and the Forest Service is not issuing any guide permits at this time. Many people who obtained them earlier are keeping a clenched fist on them, and I am not sure if they expire or can be sold or shared. A number of non-permitted tour guides have been arrested over the years, so local officials take this matter seriously. I had to bail Joint is Always Lit out of jail back in 2012; he was stepping out on his wife and taking hippie chicks skinny dipping at Grasshopper Point.

Running a retail business in Sedona is similar to many other tourist destinations. The main advantage may be that the high volume of tourists allows some clueless business owners to survive simply because so many people walk through their doors. The City of Sedona and the Sedona Chamber of Commerce heavily promote tourism, so customer volume should remain high, as long as tourists can afford to come.

The high influx of people means you can sell just about any good or service to someone. I met a guy who was making big bucks selling copper pyramids to tourists, not the huge pyramids under which you meditate, but little palm-sized pyramids. I met him in town where he was standing next to his little classic sports car. He had a table set up with a bunch of little copper pyramids selling for $150 each and they probably cost about $6 to make. When I asked what they were for, he pointed to the hood of his car. He had one mounted where a hood ornament is usually located, fastened on with only a couple of pieces of black electrical tape. It looked like a slight breeze would knock the pyramid off the car's hood. He explained to me that the pyramid increased gas mileage by as much as sixty-seven percent and he was in the process of patenting the technology. I obviously knew it was nonsense, but I asked how it worked.

He claimed, "It taps into the free energy of the earth and literally just pulls me down the road. I barely use any gas at all." I watched a couple pay cash for a pyramid, so some people actually fell for it.

I once thought that people fell for this type of stuff because they did not have access to the Internet. I met the pyramid guy before everyone had a smartphone. That however, does not explain why the Woo-Woo alarm did not go off for everyone who saw the electrical tape attachment method. But maybe that is too much to expect, considering that people have buried various crystals and stones all around Sedona to repel aliens.

One of the first people I met in Sedona was a guy named Galmetrun; I am pretty sure that was not his birth name. He lived three doors down from us in our condo complex and I often noticed a pile of red rocks on his porch. One day, I saw him taking pictures of some of the red rocks and putting them into small shipping boxes. I inquired as to what he was doing and I heard quite an earful. He was selling "Sedona Alien Vortex Rocks" online, which he gathered from a friend's backyard where a UFO supposedly shined a light on the ground. A baseball-sized rock was fetching anywhere from $50 to $75, plus shipping, and they were being shipped to his customers as far away as Europe. The kicker came when he showed me the disclaimer, which he had on his website in huge bold lettering: "For Entertainment Purposes Only. Not meant to have any effect on any type of Health Problem." Despite the clear disclaimer, his customers wrote positive reviews and testimonials of miraculous healings and huge energy surges that came from the rocks. That is the power of Red Rock Fever!

Sedona: A Place for Tree Huggers and Pavement Huggers

One of the biggest misconceptions I have heard from newcomers is the notion that Sedona will attract clientele that is largely young, single, athletic, and super spiritual. That is partially true, but some people who visit here are pavement huggers, not tree huggers. Many are middle-aged, retired, or parents with children. The fast food restaurants probably do as well as, if not better than, the vegan organic eateries.

When my life coach is not coaching me, he works in a retail shop where quite often tourists ask him for directions to the nearest food court. When he tells them the nearest restaurant is a two or three minute walk up the sidewalk, they instantly look defeated and ask if there is anywhere they can drive to. Quite seriously, they usually prefer to drive ten minutes down the road to get a fast food burger, than to walk a short distance along Uptown's main strip. Traversing crosswalks often seem like monumental feats of strength and endurance as locals try to keep their cool while tourists waddle across the street at a snail's pace.

If you wish to own and operate a retail shop that sells clothing, be aware that tourists often complain at local apparel stores that there are no 4x, 5x, or even 6x sizes available. My life coach is a t-shirt shop employee who has had to advise many customers that the 3x shirts run "small." When he sees customers who are clearly a size 6x trying to "visualize" themselves inside a 3x shirt, he knows trouble is brewing. On many occasions, customers ignored his advice only to find themselves stuck. Literally, my life coach had to call for assistance a few times when someone stuffed their 6x body inside of a 3x shirt. On the first occasion, all he could see were two arms straight up in the air, extended above the fitting room door, accompanied by a muffled plea, "Help!" The first time this happened, the customer's friend was able to remove the shirt, which by then was stretched out beyond recognition. The rescue operation took several minutes, during which the customer's arms turned purple and his face turned bright red. The purple and red customer looked like a giant finger tightly wound up with a rubber band, like what kids often do to their own fingers. Since similar bumbled rescue attempts have occurred, the store now keeps special medical shears behind the counter to cut people free. The shears worked very well, and the last I heard, employees had successfully rescued four additional customers.

Chapter 17

How I Uprooted and Transplanted to Sedona

Survival Tip: Make sure you have strong roots; love donations do not grow on trees.

      Over a decade ago, I had finished graduate school and was ready to start a public school teaching job in Massachusetts, just over the border from my home in Connecticut. Before beginning that job, I had the summer of 2007 free. A few months later, I was not only starting my career, but also getting married. It was only the two of us back then: no dogs, spirit guides, or life coaches.
      To complete the summer of 2007, one of my former college professors connected me with his church group that visited the Cheyenne River Lakota Reservation every summer. I wound up joining the group on their weeklong trip. The Lakota reservation instantly felt like home, a feeling that was replicated when I first visited my wife's family in Brazil a year and a half later. Sedona, on the other hand, took quite a few years for that feeling of home to settle in. I did not really know what the New Age was when I agreed to move here.
      While on the Lakota Reservation, many of the church members from Connecticut told me, "You have to go to Sedona." A lot of them had been all around the American West, as had I, and we exchanged many stories. They could not believe I had been almost everywhere except Sedona and the Four Corners area. Honestly, even after all the convincing, I thought Sedona sounded kind of "hokey." I was more intrigued by the Navajo and Hopi reservations.
      As fall arrived, I was married and living with my wife, and only about five minutes away from my parents. We lived on one side of a good friend's house that was divided into a duplex; my friend, his wife, and their two kids lived on the other side. My friend was an acupuncturist and a college professor, as well as an instructor of martial arts, tai chi, and qigong. In addition to being his friend and "tenant" (we were practically living rent-free but paying for utilities), I was also his martial arts student and acupuncture apprentice for quite a while. I would say he deserves

quite a bit of, if not all, the credit for keeping me out of the many "rabbit holes" Sedona has to offer. So, how did my wife and I end up living in Sedona?

My parents, also public school educators, spent their 2008 spring break vacation in Sedona. I passed on the advice that they should check out Sedona. It did not seem like I would like it, but I thought maybe my parents would. They arrived in Arizona on Sunday and called my wife and me on Thursday to let us know they had decided to retire and buy a condo in Sedona. They were hoping that we would move out west with them. The condo owner had another condo for sale and would cut us a deal for buying both. That is called RED ROCK FEVER!!!

So, my wife and I decided to uproot as well; we moved to Sedona in late July 2008, when we were both twenty-seven and had been married for just under a year. Sight unseen, we arrived in this town of extremes. The extreme beauty, personalities, ideologies, revolving door visitors, money, and the division between the haves and have nots is glaring at first. Extreme weather, in the form of searing droughts and powerful monsoon storms, presents itself every summer. Amid the Wild West spiritual playscape, there is a towering Buddhist Stupa in the heart of town, reminding us to find a middle path and stay grounded; avoiding extremes in an important principle of Buddhist philosophy.

Sedona has proven to be very unique in some aspects. While its beauty is captivating, the idea that it is overtly magical and "never meant to be lived in" appears to be a clever marketing strategy to promote mystery and intrigue. I think the reason it has taken so long for me to feel at home here is more human caused than anything else. It seems like wherever you go someone is trying to sell you something. An extreme example happened only a year and a few months after living here. I am referring to the "Sedona Sweat Lodge," where three people died in a for-profit pseudo ceremony. I was disgusted, considering that my trip to meet the Lakota people, the caretakers of the sweat lodge ceremony, is what led me to Sedona. It felt like a whirlwind of cynicism was sweeping through this town; a town I had come to with plans of living a boring life as a school teacher. Sedona had other plans for me.

Build a Solid Red Rock Foundation

What does Sedona have planned for you? Only you can find that answer. The answer may not even come from Sedona directly. I have come to see Sedona as the metaphorical center, or heart, of the New Age spiritual movement. Like anything else, there is risk and reward in "seeking." What I have found in Sedona is that the vast amount of information and different paths available for seekers can be overwhelming.

There are survival guides available for almost anything. The purpose of this book is to highlight some of the wild and crazy things that are presented in Sedona as "ancient sacred knowledge." Hopefully, with a heart opened by laughter, anyone reading this book will become aware of and avoid things like "restructured Reiki water," pseudo sweat lodges, or other dangerous activities. Humor and an open mind can establish a framework of knowledge and power on which to build a solid foundation necessary to seek safely. Seeking safely requires a hunger for knowledge, an excellent teacher, other like-minded students, and healthy experiences that will lead to life-long learning and wisdom.

The undiscerning open-mindedness of many New Age seekers makes them easy targets; victimization has become rampant and has a ripple effect. Legitimate age-old healing modalities, enlightenment paths, and traditional religious customs are often shredded and put back together into shiny new packaging. If the goal was, and sometimes is, to aide human progress, then that would be remarkable. However, usually the goal of shiny new packaging is to create a moneymaking product, not for developing empowerment or healing.

Obviously, traditional religions, paths to enlightenment, and healing modalities have been corrupted in the past, as well. The exceptional aspect of New Age fraudsters is the fact that the New Age movement was started to transcend all of that corruption, not to replicate it. Some will say I am just "hating on," "spreading fear," "being negative," "operating at a low frequency," or any other variety of hip terms to promote complacency. On the contrary, my intent is to expose how fear is used to sell New Age "products." I would agree that there are anti-New Age religious fundamentalists and zealots out there who take an extreme stance and poo-poo anything New Age. This book does not present an extreme stance whatsoever; it is as middle ground, as I think anyone will find.

If anything, I have grown to really enjoy living in Sedona where the New Age frame of mind is so prevalent. Beginning with my teenage years, I have been a huge fan of the Shaolin Temple's inclusive philosophy. The Shaolin Temple is the monastery in China that is home to the Chan Buddhist Kung Fu monks. Their policy has always been to welcome people of all faiths and backgrounds, in order to let them find their own way. They also encourage the sharing and spreading of knowledge. The entire Shaolin Temple burned down and everything was almost lost. Fortunately, five young monks preserved and kept alive most of the ancient knowledge.

I have no desire to poo-poo or dismiss the entire New Age movement. On the contrary, I think it is a great way for people to open their minds and hearts. I simply want people to have the knowledge and power needed to "navigate the minefield," so to speak. Sedona has been publically considered "super spiritual" since the Harmonic Convergence in 1987. Relatively speaking, only a few instances of tragedy have been publicized. However, there have been enough and there have been a few near misses. As mentioned earlier, on December 21, 2012, a misled group was prepared to jump off Bell Rock into a "vortex portal." Thankfully, the area was guarded by law enforcement, and what would have been a mass suicide, fell short; pun intended.

Less dramatic than the suicides, sweat lodge deaths, and sexual misconduct are the effects of fraud. Scammers waste people's time and money, which is a shame, but even worse is the stigma that consequently spreads. For example, when someone's first experience to alternative healing is with a total quack, then they will most likely get a bad taste in their mouth and perhaps turn their back on alternative medicine altogether. This collateral damage is tragic. Nothing closes hearts and minds more effectively than being ripped off by a huckster.

So how do we know which alternative healing practitioners are real and which ones are fake? That is the million-dollar question and it is necessary to do a number of litmus tests to find out. In reality, it can be very difficult to discern who is being honest and who is not. Knowledge is the best tool to build the wisdom to stay safe and avoid being ripped off along the way.

Determining who is enlightened and who is delusional can be a challenge in its own right. Many religions and cultures around the world have stories of people exhibiting behavior that in today's modern world would be labelled as mental illness. Even in modern times, people push the envelope in the name of faith; coal walking, channeling, and even handling venomous snakes are just a few examples some people will call "crazy." Again, this book cannot tell you where the edge of sanity lies. However, setting a line in the sand for yourself before you start seeking is probably a good idea.

A Lost Soul and a Fine Line Between "Enlightenment" and Mental Illness: Quandor, Emperor of Divine Wisdom

One of my favorite jokes is, "How do you make God laugh? Tell him you have a plan." You do not necessarily need a plan to get started, but having some boundaries is a good idea. For some context, I will share a quick story about someone I met in 2013 who falls into the category of "close to the edge."

I was in Uptown where I met a young gentleman from Texas who identified himself as, "Quandor, Emperor of Divine Wisdom." He was a well-groomed white man in his twenties, extremely friendly, and a little quirky. We only talked briefly, but he asked me to check out his social media page when I had a chance. He was sure I would find his posts interesting. Later that night I went online and spent about twenty minutes looking into his social media footprint. The overall message was that he was to save the world with divine wisdom that he had channeled from aliens. However, some of his videos took on a dark tone. In one clip, he was ranting about how he had the right to meditate on the sidewalk all night and no one should dare remove him or else they would, "Face the wrath of the Emperor." I noticed that he was wearing the same outfit for about three consecutive months of videos. He often live-streamed his attempts at begging for money so that he could get some fast food. The most alarming aspects were people's comments to his many videos. There were two categories: comments from friends and family back home in Texas and comments from his Sedona acquaintances.

The comments that Quandor the Emperor received from people in Texas showed that he was loved and greatly missed. People were gently telling him that he sounded like he was losing his grip on reality and that he had been doing much better in Texas until he stopped taking his prescribed medications. They had genuine concern for him and begged him to at least contact his parents, as they were worried sick about him. The Sedona comments however were quite a bit different. Quandor the Emperor was being encouraged to "continue his quest," "ignore the haters," and "continue manifesting his destiny." The only thing he was manifesting was the occasional handout that allowed him to get fast food here and there. He became very angry in one video because no one would give him money for food, and he was going to require the intervention of the aliens on his behalf. His Sedona "peeps" and enablers were nowhere to be found.

I am not a big proponent of prescription drugs, nor do I think much of western psychiatry. However, this entire story seemed like a cry for help from someone who came to Sedona as a last resort. According to Quandor's social media page, he admitted to a long-term struggle with mental illness. A few weeks passed before I saw a video of Quandor the Emperor still hanging out in Uptown. He was with a New Ager who was selling a program to train people to be "Galactic Light Warriors" in as little as a week. I have to admit, for someone I had only met briefly, I was very worried about this guy. I was put at ease when Quandor the Emperor posted a video of a surprise visitor, his brother, who came to Sedona to bring him back home. Thankfully, someone with ill intentions did not scoop up Quandor the Emperor, and his family was willing to come help him. My goal is not to embarrass or single out Quandor the Emperor; there have probably been countless other people in Sedona with similar stories. I just think his story is a cautionary one and a good example of someone "getting lost when trying to find himself."

Anyhow, I do not think Sedona or the New Age movement is "past the point of no return." I actually think that things may turn around eventually. People are getting smarter and the Internet, especially social media, is shedding a lot of light on areas that were previously in the dark.

Hopefully, in the near future people will help balance one another with reason.

The Future of Sedona

In the past ten years, Sedona has become eerily similar to places like Jamaica where huge mansions line the hillsides, and tin fishing shacks crowd the streets and beaches. The landscape and feel of the town really changed in 2016 when Arizona passed a short-term rental law, SB 1350, which has greatly increased housing costs and shrunk the long-term rental market. In years past, the houses on the hill in Sedona were reserved for the rich. Middle class folks could afford renting a small house or even a mobile home in less desirable locations. Not anymore! Now, single-family homes, even very run-down mobile homes, have been turned into short-term rentals. Investors are buying up properties as soon as they are available, and long-term tenants are being pushed out of the rental market.

Very diverse groups of long-term residents tie in with the theme of extreme opposites. Many retired, refined, conservative folks live here who simply want to play golf, host grandkids, and maybe sip wine and watch the sunset over the red rocks. There is also quite a large community of people who have been affectionately (or not so affectionately) referred to as the Woo-Woos. These are the UFO-obsessed folks, psychics, mediums, healers, and "trustafarians." Trustafarians? Actually, that is a term from about six years ago when dread locks were still trendy among the hippie crowd and when this hippie crowd consisted of the trust fund kids who were able to "retire" at a young age on their parent's generosity and just kind of chill out in Sedona. The last group is composed of long-term business owners who have been fortunate enough to create and build successful businesses in this town.

The people in the middle, the younger people (without a trust fund), just cannot make it anymore. School enrollment is way down; so much so that Big Park School in VOC recently had to close its doors. The future of Sedona seems to be headed further towards the paradigm of extreme populations, with an ever-dwindling middle class to balance it out.

Little by little, the middle class is being moved out of the area. Short-term rentals and expensive retirement homes will probably be all that is left in the not so distant future. I do not think there will be very many people under the age of sixty-five living here ten years from now. As a result, Sedona is really losing a big chunk of its soul. I was lucky enough to move here before its death throes. Living here has been like meeting a friend who knows they are dying, yet is desperately trying to make everyone around them happy for as long as possible. Many of us who live here have gone through the stages of grief already; yet, some are still in the denial stage and many are in the anger stage. One thing is for sure: unless you have a VIP pass on an interdimensional time machine, there is no going back to the Sedona of yesterday.

Afterward

     As I was finishing this book, I spoke with a friend of mine from back east. He is a UFO fanatic who came out to Sedona a few years ago, who was in paradise during his time here. It was as if he was on a pilgrimage to the Promised Land. Ever since then, he has been dying to get back here for a visit. For him, moving here would be like winning the New Age lottery. As I explained the concept for this book to him, he asked, "What is a Woo-Woo?" That is when I realized I had lived in Sedona for too long!

     Our conversation really opened my eyes to how much we transplants take this place for granted. Sure, traffic can be bad and the town is getting crowded, but it is an incredible place. There is always something new to see, no matter how many times you visit or how long you live here.

     I think my friend's wife put it best when we were sitting under a starry Sedona sky a few years ago. She poetically exclaimed to her husband, "Living in Sedona has been kind of like being married to you for the past twenty-five years. At first, I had to pinch myself every day to make sure I was not dreaming. I mean, you are so handsome and charming, but then I got used to it all. Now, the only time I remember how lucky I am, is whenever we are out on the town and I see braless hippie ladies in yoga pants undressing you with their eyes, just like I used to do."

Extended Glossary (Super Spiritual Version)

The Long Version of Essential Sedona Survival Terms / Guru-splaining: (super spiritual slang words and phrases translated to layman's terms)

This glossary is not in astrological or alphabetical order. Instead, one term flows into the next, in a synchronized cosmic event. This glossary is meant to be read start to finish, as the definitions flow into one another… Enjoy!

Astrology – New Age astronomy

Grounded – sober

Protected – really, really, high

Elders – senior citizens

Ancestors – no one is really sure

Crystal in the Toot Chakra – New Age equivalent of a stick up your ass

Bra – an ancient artifact, last one seen in Sedona was sometime in 1997

Cord Cutting – New Age version of getting rid of a loser boyfriend

Twin Flames – boyfriend and girlfriend. Alternate meaning – smoking two joints at once.

Soul Mates – New Age couple that made it past the fourth date

Sacred Geometry – Polyamorous New Age love triangle

Singing Bowls – magical bowls that emit different frequencies and transform cereal into manna from heaven

Gong – a musical instrument used to summon spirits and create a "sacred transformational space." Not to be confused with a bong.

Sacred Transformational Space – kind of like a safe space for New Agers

Bong – a water pipe for smoking ganja

Ganja – reefer

Reefer – herb

Herb – wacky tobbacky

Wacky Tobbacky – the chronic

The Chronic – Mary Jane

Mary Jane – icky sticky

Icky Sticky – medicinal

Medicinal – 420

420 – leafy green goodness

Leafy Green Goodness - bud

Bud – marijuana

Marijuana – see above…

Pot – metal container to cook marijuana butter or another word for marijuana

Toke – inhalation of marijuana

Peaceful energy – making love, not war

Manifesting – wishing for someone to do it for you: the universe, a friend, or whoever is listening

Focus on the positive – stick your head in the sand and hope passers-by respect the "Exit Only" sign on your backside

Shift – a change in behavior or spirit purpose

Spirit purpose – something that sounds like a good idea while high

Ancient Alchemy – beer before liquor, you have never been sicker. Liquor before beer, you are in the clear bliss of radiant energy and divine presence.

Gratitude – a mini Thanksgiving with crystals and maybe even a Tofu Turkey

Dolphin People – a wet and wild good time

Psychics – best paid educated guessers in the world

Starseed – New Age sales pitch aimed at "proving" intergalactic reincarnation of aliens on earth

Manifesting Abundance – sooner you get paid, sooner you get laid

Radiating Love and Light – being in a good mood

Resonate – agree with or attracted to an idea

Sacred Space – depending on context, might be located in the nether regions where the sun don't shine

Receiving – listening

Reiki – energy landscapers

Yoga – a class guys take to pick up chicks

Synchronicity – when you always poop before your shower

Energy Stagnation – when you have to poop after your shower

Tatanka (Buffalo) Chips – polite New Age way of saying bullshit

Bullshit – something common, widespread, and deep in the New Age, like spiritual quicksand.

Breatharianism – a perfect example of bullshit

Gluten – New Age equivalent of devil food

Gluten-free – food that has had the demons cast out

Vegan – someone who is so spiritual, their farts smell like roses and sunshine

Vegan Diet – the only way to reach Nirvana

Nirvana – somewhere over the rainbow, turn left at the first vortex

Vortex – too mysterious to define

Aligned – remembered to shave and brush teeth this morning

Energy is Off – in need of a nap

Planets are in Retrograde – an excuse to act all crazy

Yurt – a backyard playhouse for adults

Alien-Hybrid Children – result of getting jiggy during an alien abduction

Soul Retrieval – spiritual lost and found

Shame-Men – make-believe Shaman

Pretendian – Non-Native Americans with made-up names like Balding Eagle or Who Stepped on Frog

Lightworker – someone whose karma cannot handle the night shift

Empath – someone who will make you roll your eyes

Sensitive – someone even Empaths will rolls their eyes at

Chemically Sensitive – runs around naked after a single shot of vodka or two beers

Chakra – Seven depositories in the body that collect and store energy from the seven spiritual food groups

Seven Spiritual Food Groups – Marijuana, Ayahausca, Magic Mushrooms, Peyote, San Pedro Cactus, Ecstasy, and LSD

Akashic Records – a library in the sky; no library card needed, just a bit of Ayahausca

Ayahausca – Ecstasy for tree huggers

Inner Child – that fun loving voice inside you that tells you to skip work and get high instead

Channeling – getting in touch with your inner child in order to reconnect with imaginary friends from childhood

Spirit Animal – little hidden creatures that reveal themselves through marijuana smoke

Aura – the proximity around someone where you can smell their body odor, receive messages from their spirit guides, or get a contact-high

Spirit Guides – tour guides who work for secondhand marijuana smoke

Orbs – solidified marijuana smoke that floats around

The Veil – A metaphysical wall that President Trump built in a past life to stop spiritual travelers from traveling to the astral plane

Astral Plane – a non-stop, round trip flight to the spirit world and back

Past Life – a make-believe story to create a New Age persona

Contemplation – unrealistic thoughts of getting something done when too high to move

Sage Smudging or Cleansing – a smoke shower; give them credit, most hippies do not shower at all

Karmic Residue – an STD that the soul catches

Out-of-Body Experience – aliens made me do it

Near Death Experience – what happens if you smoke all of your girlfriend's weed without replacing it

Dharma – kind of like Karma, but groovier

Karma – when you are a jerk to someone, trust a fart, and realize you sharted in your pants.

Sharted – worst of both worlds, the moonchild of a shit and a fart

Moonchild – end result of a full moon, two horny hippies, a bag of magic mushrooms, and lack of foresight to buy condoms

Foresight – way more spiritual than the less evolved third eye

Third Eye – extra sensory ability that your girlfriend uses to catch you looking at porn or texting random girls

Extra Sensory – a downloaded cosmic upgrade to heighten your abilities

Cosmic Upgrade – a major improvement to the pilot of your meat suit

Download – a direct telepathic message from aliens

Abilities – usually made-up nonsense

Telepathic – the spiritual communication ability that makes cell phones seem passé and irrelevant

Meat Suit – the uncomfortable outfit you were born in that keeps your spirit from higher truth and epiphanies

Epiphany – a New Ager who lost her psychic abilities and became a stripper

Great Awakening – result of ingesting an entire bag of magic mushrooms

Enlightened – read a bunch of yoga magazines, bought some crystals, and got a massage. Also, learned how to talk with eyes closed, very slowly and quietly.

New Age Hug - super long, super uncomfortable invasion of space, may or may not have some eye gazing thrown in for good measure

Eye Gazing – trying to get someone pregnant, or give an orgasm by simply staring into her eyes. Very similar phenomena to a staring contest, but much more spiritually advanced.

Ascended – went on a make-believe vacation to talk with imaginary friends

Faith Healing – praying that your massage therapist does not like to play grab ass, give unwanted happy endings, or yoni massages

Happy Ending – a leading cause of divorce among massage parlor enthusiasts

Yoni Massage – sexual assault during a massage, with a super spiritual name as a disguise

Yoni – a va jay jay

Va Jay Jay – a vagina

Lingam – a ding dong

Ding Dong - a penis

Prostate Massage – self-explanatory, kind of like a "New Age physical"

Dakini / Daka – female and male names for New Age, often geriatric, nymphomaniac tantric practitioners

Tantric Practitioner – horny New Ager

Tantric Partner – New Age booty call, friend with benefits

Tantric Practice – getting laid in the New Age

Moon Time – a magical time of introspection to get together with other New Age women and braid each other's armpit hair

Reflexology – a foot massage that targets points which correspond to different parts of the body. Very little risk of an unwanted happy ending or yoni massage.

Acupuncture – a therapeutic way to turn your body into a voodoo doll. Based upon Traditional Chinese Medicine that is thousands of years old.

Goddess – most New Age women

God – Creator of the universe who shakes his head every time a New Age guy with a sarong and a man bun tries to convince hippie chicks that *he is a god*

Sarong – a spiritual skirt for men with man buns

Man Bun – Kind of like a sensitive and fashion forward Samurai Warrior topknot. Also serves as an insurance policy for men who are afraid of attracting a woman with self-respect.

Free Spirit – Someone who wants to just chill out on the river of life and allow others to pay their way while they "find themselves"

Finding One's self – a journey many have attempted, only never to be seen or heard from again

Self-help – phenomenon of paying lots of money for someone to tell you to get off the couch

Hairy Legs – commonplace on women ever since a guru proclaimed, "No one will say burr, if their legs are full of fur"

Guru – those who cannot do, coach life

Life Coach – a way to make money by giving advice that the giver of said advice should follow

Hairy Armpits on Women – sometimes even braided with beads, makes a really nice pillow for the evolved New Age man

Emotions – provide proof and affirmations

Affirmations – hearing exactly what you want to hear

A Feeling – New Age equivalent of proof

Rational Thought – not sure, been in Sedona too long

Scientific Proof – "the Man" trying to oppress us

Logic – New Age blasphemy

Reason – usually do not need one, if you got it, smoke it

Flat Earth Theory – belief that the earth is flat. New Age version of the Old Testament. The stupidest thing ever to go viral.

Mandela Effect – Belief in alternate timelines and dimensions. New Age version of the New Testament. Runner-up for the stupidest thing ever to go viral.

Mantra – repeating something over and over again with the end goal of never needing a shopping list again

Meditation – closing your eyes in public and making weird noises so people will be uncomfortable and leave you alone, so that you can enjoy the after effects of your joint

Joint – marijuana cigarette

Prayer – asking the universe for money

New Age Church – too broad to define

Pay-to-Play Sweat Lodge – a way for New Agers to get lots of green energy by selling a Lakota ceremony

Lakota – a Native American tribe from the Great Plains, with an unusually high rate of reincarnation in Sedona

Sacrilegious – pointing out anything negative, only positive thoughts permitted

Chi – energy, kind of like prana

Prana – energy, kind of like kundalini

Kundalini – a little snake that lives in your butt just waiting to wake you up

Revelation – those annoying moments of clarity when you run out of weed

Yin and Yang – opposing forces, opposite to the law of attraction

Law of Attraction – if you drink enough gluten-free beer on St. Patrick's Day, leprechauns will lead you to a pot of gold, somewhere in Sacred Sedona

Sacred – everything, except negativity

Sedona – a magical place where the law of the land is attraction. You are about to receive more than you may be ready to download and the energy may be too powerful for your aura to handle. Make sure those chakras are aligned, the vortexes are waiting…

One Last Thing

In the Preface of this book, I promised that I would not again enter the realm of seriousness. My intention was to keep that promise, until I recently received some tragic news: A young man, who could be described as the mirror image of Quandor the Emperor from Chapter 17, took his own life. Like Quandor, he believed he was a Messiah; he was a self-proclaimed "savior" and "holy man." He also admitted to be suffering from the same mental illness as Quandor. At first glance, he seemed like a vibrant free spirit, just floating down the river of life. However, his yoga obsession, world travels, and lavish lifestyle left him penniless and homeless. Unfortunately, as he was trying to save the world, there was no one to save him.

This news upset me because I hurt when I witness suffering, and especially death, among spiritual seekers. My intent with sharing the silly stories in this book is to help us lighten up, but also to prevent tragedies, like Quandor's and this young man's, from happening. The news also struck close to home; even though I never attempted suicide, I almost lost my life while seeking spiritual enlightenment. Years before the infamous "Sedona Sweat Lodge Incident," I escaped severe injury and death in a mismanaged sweat lodge ceremony. Somehow, I survived with my life and sense of humor intact.

Throughout this book, I have alluded to my multiple Near Death Experiences and subsequent interest in spirituality. Also, I am an enthusiastic student of world religions. For years, I have felt distressed to see the corruption, fraud, and sexual abuse occurring not only in organized religious institutions, but also in the New Age culture. I have found that the hypocrisy of organized religions, along with cultural appropriation, have influenced the New Age to essentially morph into another for-profit religion.

My desire is to shed light on the destructive underbelly of New Age culture. As such, and in light of mentioned tragedies, I have important information and perspectives that I wish to share in my upcoming book entitled: *Sedona Heart of the New Age: Prophets and Profits.*

I still believe the best way to open minds is to first open hearts. I hope you enjoyed the wild ride you just went on while reading this book. I also hope it meant more to you than just a mere collection of absurd stories and juvenile toilet humor. If I was able to open your heart with laughter, even a little bit, then I hope you will join me on my next journey. It is a much more serious book; however, I saved quite a few wild, wacky, and humorous stories for that adventure as well.

Thank you for reading…

Made in the USA
Columbia, SC
27 February 2019